AF528344

A Career in the Sky

Megha Madan has been an international flight attendant for over a decade now. She still craves the excitement her job brings as much as she did when she was new to it. It is equal parts rewarding and stressful and she loves every bit of it.

She hails from Shivpuri, a small town in Madhya Pradesh, India.

Presently, she lives in Delhi with her husband and six-year-old son, Daksh, who is equally passionate about airplanes. When Megha is not travelling around the world, she spends most of her time with her family.

Despite being a part of one of the most glamorous industries in the world, she believes in simplicity and good old hard work. She hasn't forgotten her roots and that is what surprises people the most.

A Career in the Sky

YOUR
STEP-BY-STEP
GUIDE TO BECOMING A
FLIGHT ATTENDANT

Megha Madan

AMARYLLIS

AMARYLLIS

An imprint of Manjul Publishing House Pvt. Ltd.
• C-16, Sector 3, Noida, Uttar Pradesh 201301, India
Website: www.manjulindia.com

Registered Office:
• 2nd Floor, Usha Preet Complex, 42 Malviya Nagar, Bhopal 462 003 – India

Distribution Centres
Ahmedabad, Bengaluru, Chennai, Kochi, Kolkata, Hyderabad, Mumbai, New Delhi, Pune

A Career in the Sky: Your Step-by-Step Guide to Becoming a Flight Attendant by Megha Madan

Copyright © Megha Madan, 2021

Megha Madan asserts the moral right to be identified as the author of this work

This edition first published in India in 2021
Second impression 2025

ISBN 978-93-91242-86-2

Cover design by Wasim Helal

Printed and bound in India by Repro India Limited

This book is designed to provide information. The content of the book is the sole expression and opinion of its author, and not that of the publisher. No warranties or guarantees are expressed or implied by the publisher's choice to include any of the content in this volume. Neither the publisher nor the author shall be liable for any physical, psychological, emotional, financial, or commercial damages, including but not limited to, special, incidental, consequential or other damages.

All rights reserved. No part of this book may be used or reproduced, stored in or introduced into a retrieval system, or transmitted, in any form, or by any means (electronic, mechanical, photocopying, recording or otherwise) without the prior written permission of the Publisher. Any person who does any unauthorized act in relation to this publication may be liable to criminal prosecution and civil claims for damages.

This book is dedicated to:

The most important pillars of my life – my parents – who supported me unconditionally through thick and thin. They gave me the freedom to take my decisions and accepted them wholeheartedly. They are full of life, and this is something I am still learning from them.

My sister, who motivated me to strive harder every time I failed. Being a social development professional, she always showed me the positive side of my dream job, which seemed rare in those days.

My brother, the most positive and zealous person in our family. Despite being so young, he has taught me valuable lessons to remain happy and grateful.

My husband, who has been the inspiration behind this book. He supported me to sustain my career by sharing the workload, and most importantly, by babysitting at home while I was at work.

My sunshine, my cute little son, Daksh, who grew wiser and faster for his age; and has adapted to living without his mother so often and still manages to be happy.

And finally to my Pilot, Lord Shiva, whose blessings have been a guiding light in my life. He has been my biggest source of strength in the most challenging situations.

He was the only one holding my hand while I was away from my family and friends. I shared all my sorrows and happiness with Him. I got the power to perform and accomplish. I thank you, God, for all the love and courage.

Contents

Acknowledgements

I wish with all my heart that this book will be of help to all the people who aspire to be cabin crew. The book throws light on the profession and the duties of cabin crew, as well as the necessary procedures that one has to go through in order to have this extraordinary career.

This guidebook will help you decide whether this profession is for you. It will also make you fit for it.

I have made all possible efforts to amass information that will help you understand everything that is to know about a career in the sky. I have provided practical advice and real insights into what it takes to enter and progress in this profession.

I would like to express my gratitude towards my parents who keep inspiring me. Their faith and support gave me the courage to pursue my dream. Whoever I am today is because of them and their confidence in me. I will always remain indebted to them.

I would like to thank my friends and colleagues who helped make this book better by giving valuable counsel and advice. I'm particularly grateful to Amardeep K. Singh, without whom some chapters wouldn't have been possible.

I would also like to thank my critics whose constructive and helpful assessment made me work harder.

And above all, I am grateful to Lord Shiva, my pilot, who always guides me in the right direction.

Finally, I would like to thank all my readers for accepting this book as their mentor. Let's begin!

Introduction

Dear future flight attendant,

Congratulations on taking the first step towards fulfilling your dream of becoming a flight attendant!

You need to overcome many challenges that life will throw at you when you decide to pursue your ambitions. However, know that challenges always teach us important life lessons that propel us forward in our endeavours. What we need to do when these obstacles come in our path is stand tall and face them.

This profession certainly sounds and seems glamorous. One gets paid to jet across continents, live in plush hotels and meet and interact with people from all over the world. But getting this job is no easy feat. This isn't just a job, it's a lifestyle! It demands a new version of yourself that can distinctively stand apart in a crowd. For this, you need a smarter approach to the process. With a lot of preparation and perseverance you can get there.

It is a fact that only 5 out of 100 applicants get shortlisted. After reading this, you must be wondering whether you even stand a chance then? But the good news is that the 5 candidates who get shortlisted are those who give it their all and do extremely well.

If you too wish to be among the privileged 5, consider this book as your guide. The more prepared you are, the better your chances of selection!

It is, of course, a lot of hard work. Hence, I am here to help you and tell you everything I know from my own experience. I will walk you through the entire process that will help you fulfill your lifelong dream. This is a step-by-step guide. All you need to do is follow the steps.

Now you must be wondering: Why should I believe anything that is written in this book?

I have been flying as an international flight attendant for over a decade now. I hail from a small town and have a humble background. So it was not at all easy for me to enter this adventurous profession. Having faced and overcome many challenges throughout my journey, I have gained immense knowledge and experience, and that is what I'll pass on to you through this book.

It is said that our thoughts set our behaviour, our behaviour creates some actions and our actions bring results.

Now ask yourself a question: Would you like to be a part of a profession that will make you financially sound, pay for your stay in luxury hotels, and make you travel around the world among other things?

Doesn't that sound amazing? I'm sure you agree. But, how will you get there? Trust me, it seemed unbelievable when I thought about it for the first time. Believe it or not, that life is within your reach. I want you to make a commitment to yourself that you will become a flight attendant no matter what it takes. Say this out loud to yourself at least 5 times a day: 'I am committed to becoming a flight attendant, no matter what. I will not give up.'

Bravo! How does that feel? Isn't it invigorating? Repeat the above sentence for 5 minutes every day.

The fact that you are reading this book is proof enough that you are passionate about taking up this career. This book will be a worthy companion on your successful journey.

The First Stepping Stones to Success in the Sky

Have Faith in Yourself and the Divine

I firmly believe that nothing happens without a reason. Whenever something good is supposed to happen, it appears in the form of intentions in front of us. Our intentions pave the way for our reality.

There is a saying, 'Your faith can move mountains'. Hence, you must have complete faith in your abilities and persevere, no matter what.

Once you start believing in yourself and have faith in the divine, you will find ways and means to reach your goal. Everything will fall into place when you start working towards your goal diligently. I am saying this from personal experience. You are always guided intuitively towards your destination when you let the divine become the pilot of your life.

Knowledge and Skills Increase Confidence

The more knowledge and skills you have, the more confident you will be, and the better chance you will have at excelling in several aspects of your life.

Ways to improve your knowledge and skills:

- Research about the field. Read everything you can get your hands on.
- Read extensively. Enhance your vocabulary.
- Subscribe to relevant newsletters and magazines.
- Listen to insightful audiobooks.
- Talk to experienced professionals from the industry.
- Watch YouTube videos that give advise, information and tips.
- Join courses to enhance your communication and customer service skills.
- Work on having proper command on the language. Being fluent in English is a huge asset.
- Stand in front of the mirror and practice. English songs, shows and movies can also aid in improving your language skills.
- Work on your body language. It speaks for you.

I worked as a customer service representative at a five star hotel for more than a year. The experience I gained there helped me to a great extent during the several interviews I gave after applying for flight attendant vacancies at various airlines. Many a times I found myself losing confidence especially when I faced rejections. However, I did not let the lack of confidence affect me. After every interview, I tried to get some feedback, did self-analysis and worked upon my weaknesses so that I could be better prepared for the next interview.

If you are passionate about your goal and give it your all, nothing can stop you from achieving what you want. Think about your dream and imagine you're living it.

There is a secret behind this phenomenon of living your dream in your mind. They say when you start imagining it, you work even harder to achieve your dream. You also send out a clear message to the universe that you are passionate about your goal and that you will do everything in your power to get there. When I did it, trust me, I had no clue on how this phenomenon worked. I didn't realise that our mind works like a magnet.

Steps to Becoming a Flight Attendant

Requirements

Let's talk about the specific requirements that are stipulated for flight attendants. These play a key role in deciding who gets the job. Every airline has its way of conducting interviews but basic requirements are the same everywhere. The reason behind this is that they are all monitored by an airline regulatory body which is country specific. In India, the regulatory body for civil aviation is The Directorate General of Civil Aviation (DGCA). Then, there is the International Civil Aviation Organization (ICAO). Its primary role is to provide a set of standards which help regulate aviation across the world. Apart from these, a few airlines may have some additional requirements as well. Let's have a look at some of the prerequisites:

Age

Age is not just a number here, unfortunately. The minimum age requirement to apply for the job of a flight attendant in India is 18 years, and 21 years or above in some international airlines.

However, there is no age limit in some American and European airline companies. If one is fit and healthy, and is passionate about this industry, they can apply for this job. This is applicable for the candidates living in those places or having a work visa and permit to live in that country.

Unfortunately, this isn't the norm in India. In our country the age limit varies when it comes to the newcomers and experienced people. For beginners, the age limit is 18-28. Whereas, experienced candidates should be 30 years and above. Veteran candidates who have ample flying experience are preferred.

When I applied to be a flight attendant, the age criteria for newcomers was 18-23 years. This made me anxious as I was close to the maximum age bar. But fortunately, my passion and determination paid off and at last, I ended up getting my dream job.

Height

One is required to mention one's height in the resume. Candidates are only called for the interview when they meet the height criteria. If it is an open day or walk-in interview, height is measured in the first round of interviews. The minimum height requirement for women is 155 cm when it comes to domestic airlines in India and it's 157 cm and above for international airlines. For the male candidates, the requirement is 165-170 cm. However, it may vary depending on the airlines. There is a physical standard as well that the assessors look for. The physical reach requirement is 212 cm. An important distinction needs to be made here. This is not a height requirement. It is a reach requisite. You may be on the shorter side, but if you have long arms and can touch a marker at 212 cm when you are standing on your toes, then you meet the minimum standards. Some airlines are lenient when it comes to this and some aren't. You must always check the eligibility and requirements before applying anywhere.

Weight

Your weight should be in proportion to your height. You should not be overweight or underweight. The body mass index should be 18 to 22 for women and 18 to 25 for men. This may differ from airline to airline.

If you have a few weeks' time before open day, you can actually make significant progress by minding your diet and working out. Can there be a better motivation for improving your health and fitness levels than your dream job waiting for you?

Vision

The acceptable vision for this job is 20/40 with glasses or contact lenses. You do not need to have a 20/20 vision to qualify for the position. An applicant should wear his corrective lenses or glasses while taking the vision test. Some airlines also accept candidates with glasses. You will undergo a medical test in which your eyesight will be tested.

Swimming

Major international airlines fly over the sea or other water bodies; hence, swimming is a required skill. Some airlines keep this test in the first round as a lot of candidates clear the other rounds but fail when it comes to this. However, domestic airlines in India do not have a swimming test.

I would highly recommend you learn swimming. You should not miss any opportunity that would raise the bar in your favour. This skill can come in handy any time.

If you apply at an international airline, you will be asked to swim 50 metres or the entire length of the swimming pool, unattended.

Medical Test

The last round of the interview will be a medical test. Before an airline hires you, you need to undergo a full body check-up to determine whether you are fit for the job or not. This job requires high levels of energy and physical fitness. This test includes all types of blood tests, a urine test, an ultrasound, an x-ray, eye test, hearing test, cancer test and more.

Grooming for Female Candidates

Grooming plays an integral role in the airline industry. Airlines are very particular about the appearance of cabin crew and you must look the part. There are some standards that need to be adhered to. You should be just as well-groomed as the cabin crew you see. This is imperative. You cannot be sloppy when it comes to how you look. The most important thing is that you should be confident in your skin. Body language speaks for itself. Anything you wear wouldn't look good if you're not exuding confidence.

Here are some standard requirements:

- **Hair** – Hair should be tied up neatly in a bun or a pony tail. Your face should be clearly visible. See which style suits you best and decide accordingly. Practice by watching tutorials, if necessary, and perfect your style. Hair colour should be natural and if coloured, it should be in neutral colours. Streaks or bright shades like reds, pinks, etc., should be strictly avoided. Hair spray and gel that have a strong scent or odour should be avoided as well. Avoid using clips and pins.
- **Makeup** – You must follow the golden rule of makeup: Don't overdo it and don't downplay it. Go with the 'no makeup' makeup look. It should look effortless even though we all know a lot of time and effort goes into pulling off a simple look. Know your skin type. Use good products, eat healthy, exercise and keep yourself hydrated. If you feel good about yourself, you will look confident. Cleaning, toning and moisturizing is a must before applying any makeup. Apply some base or primer before applying makeup as well.

  Use a good concealer to get an even tone. Some light eye makeup will enhance your eyes. Shades of nude, pink, peach and brown would look just right. You must wear a nice shade of long-lasting lipstick. Reds and pinks are recommended. Loud makeup should be avoided. A good fragrance is a must but the perfume shouldn't be overpowering either.
- **Jewellery** – Do not wear large hoops or dangling earrings. Wear tiny studs, if necessary. Pearl earrings look graceful. Nose rings, eyebrow rings, more than two earrings or costume jewellery are a strict no-no. One or two rings on the finger can be worn. A nice wristwatch will complete your look.
- **Outfit** – The right outfit plays a very important role in making an impression. The standard dress code for female candidates is a suit and skirt. Wear a formal suit or a blouse with a jacket and skirt or trousers. You cannot go wrong with blacks, greys, blues or browns. The shirt should be a cotton or silk blend material. The colours should never be loud.

Investing in a well-tailored suit will pay later.

If you wear a skirt, it should not be too tight or too short. A knee-length skirt is ideal.

The blouse should be well-ironed and fit comfortably. A square scarf will enhance the look. Your stockings should be nude or should match your skin tone.

- **Tattoos** – Any visible tattoos are not allowed. They may act as a deterrent to your being selected. Airlines are very particular about this. However, some airlines don't object unless your tattoo is visible.
- **Nails** – Hands are visible at all times so do not ignore your nails. Getting a manicure done before the interview is advisable. French tips or neutral shades are ideal. Avoid bright, loud nail paints. Nails should not be too long.
- **Shoes** – Formal shoes in neutral shades that compliment your outfit should be worn. Medium heels are advisable. Do not wear open-toe shoes, high boots or casual footwear. Avoid anything that is flashy and loud.

Grooming for Male Candidates

- **Hair** – Hair should be nicely trimmed and preferably short. You can use gel to make your hair look well-styled.
- **Facial Hair** – Most airlines prefer a clean-shaven look. Some airlines also allow a trimmed beard. The rules vary. However, it is advisable to sport a clean-shaven look for the interview irrespective of the airline.
- **Attire** – Formals are the best choice when it comes to the interview. Dark, deep colours like black, grey, blue look just right.
- **Ties** – Wear a simple, solid-colour tie. It should not be flashy. Ties with images, loud patterns or designer logos should be avoided. The tie should complement your attire.
- **Socks** – Choose a colour that coordinates with your suit.

- **Shoes** – Wear formal shoes; black or brown. Make sure they are properly polished and clean. Avoid sports shoes, boots or any sort of casual footwear.
- **Jewellery and cologne** – Do not wear more than one ring. And avoid wearing earrings at all costs. Wear an elegant wristwatch as that would help in making a good impression. Wear a cologne that isn't overpowering.

Key Attributes

There are certain key attributes that are necessary in order to be able to perform smoothly and efficiently. All you need to do is practise, be consistent and work hard. This will help you master the required skills well in time. Remember there is always scope for improvement. You know what they say: Practise makes perfect.

The most important attributes that airlines look for in candidates are:

- **Communication skills** – As a flight attendant you will get to meet and interact with a lot of people from all around the world. It's important to be fluent in English and other necessary languages. Having a good command over languages will help you a great deal. You can work on improving your communication skills by practising in front of the mirror, listening to podcasts and trying to speak in a similar manner. But do not imitate. You have your own style. Embrace it. Movies, shows and songs help as well. Make practising English fun and you will get better in no time.
- **Flexibility** – You may or may not get leave on festivals, birthdays or anniversaries. This will be difficult so you'll have to mentally prepare yourself for times like these when you won't be able to be with your family and friends. Also, at times you will have to fly short-haul flights covering less than 3 hours of distance, and at times you will have to fly long-haul flights covering 6-12 hours of distance. They may be in different geographical locations too. Thus, you need to learn to go with the flow.

- **Customer service skills** – As a flight attendant, your job will be to ensure the safety of the passengers, and give them a better flying experience by offering them great customer service. Your duties will include greeting passengers and ensuring they are properly seated, serving food and refreshments, conducting regular cabin and cockpit checks, restocking supplies, keeping an eye on the passengers in case they need anything, among other things. Hence, you must always be friendly, caring and courteous. Keeping a cool head under any and every circumstance is a must.
- **Language skills** – If you can speak any other regional or foreign language, that is an added advantage. Some airlines may also require you to speak regional languages other than your mother tongue.
- **Handling pressure** – Flight attendants work in all kinds of weather conditions and time zones. They work odd and long hours. And they're always under some or the other kind of pressure. Keeping a cool head isn't optional here. Roughly speaking, there must be one flight attendant for fifty passengers. To deal with so many people one needs to possess certain abilities. Emergencies come unannounced. Flight attendants have to keep their wits about them and work through any kind of stressful situation. One has to be prepared to deal with medical emergencies, difficult passengers, safety issues and so much more.
- **Decision-making skills** – During their entire career, flight attendants face many familiar and unfamiliar situations wherein they have to take prompt decisions. Being quick on your feet and taking decisions in all kinds of situations is an art that can be learned with training.
- **Handling difficult situations** – Do you panic when you have to face any challenge? If yes, this is one aspect you must work on. As a flight attendant, you will be required to handle many difficult situations such as dealing with fussy passengers, unforeseen medical issues or safety hazards, planned or

unplanned emergencies, etc. Your ability to keep a cheery countenance during distressing work hours will make you a competent cabin crew member.

- **Team player** – You will always have to work with other crew members. On a flight you do not work just as an individual. Good team players are committed, reliable and responsible. They are active listeners. They support and respect other members of the team and work together in harmony. If you aren't a team player, either you will have to learn how to become one or give up on your dream of becoming a flight attendant.
- **Patience** – How patient are you? This job demands an extremely high level of patience. Dealing with all sorts of passengers in varied situations is challenging, to say the least, and this job will test your patience all the time. Patience is therefore going to be one of your key assets. Learn to *respond* to situations in a calm manner, and not *react*.
- **Positive attitude** – As this is a very hands-on and stressful job, people who sport a positive attitude are the ones who are able to excel. Airlines prefer such candidates. A smile on your face will take you a long way.
- **Punctuality** – Every flight has fixed timings for takeoffs and landings. You are always supposed to reach the airport before the scheduled time so that you can prepare for the flight. You can get calls at odd hours, so you must be prepared to leave at a moment's notice.

Other Requirements

- **Educational qualifications** – Any applicant who has passed higher secondary is eligible to apply. Having a college degree would be an added advantage.
- **Passport** – You must have a passport that is valid for at least 6 months to 1 year. If you don't, apply for one immediately.

Roles and Responsibilities

Flight attendants need to be hard-working, disciplined and dedicated. They need to remain vigilant and attentive all the time. The job of a flight attendant carries a huge amount of responsibility. It is both physically demanding and mentally taxing. They are responsible for the well-being and the safety of the passengers. Further, they need to take care of all the passengers' requests on board. Here are some of the tasks that flight attendants are required to perform:

- **Safety procedure** – The primary responsibility of a flight attendant is to ensure a safe flight for the passengers. This includes a hands-on demonstration of safety and security procedures in order to help passengers understand where emergency equipments are placed before take-off. This avoids last-minute panic in case of an accident. As a flight attendant, prepare to repeat instructions multiple times.
- **Aircraft security search** – You have to search the entire cabin and galleys to ensure no items are left behind by the passengers or any staff.
- **Inspection** – As soon as you are on board, you will have to check your assigned station to make certain that each and every equipment is in place, and in working condition. If not, you are required to report this to your senior.
- **Monitoring passengers** – You have to be present in the cabin during boarding to not only welcome the passengers but to also keep an eye on their activities, in case of unusual behaviour. One of the assigned crew has to count the passengers to avoid

any discrepancy. It's important to stay active and vigiliant at all times.

- **Special passengers** – Extra care and attention must be given to passengers on wheelchairs, the elderly, infants, unaccompanied minors, differently abled, etc. There is a safety briefing which you need to give to these passengers or their caregivers for handling an emergency situation.
- **Customer service** – Excellent customer service entails tact and resourcefulness when dealing with customers' needs. Based on the allocation of your work, you will have to serve the passengers on different tiers: first class, business class, or economy class. Maintain a kind demeanour at all times and serve the customer with a smile every time they press the bell. At the end of the day, you must be able to provide a pleasant and stress-free travel experience.

Salary, Allowances and Perks

There's always a heightened sense of curiosity and excitement for discovering the various perks and allowances that come along with this fabulous job. Without further ado, let's take a look at the salaries and other add-ons across airlines:

- **Salary** – Your salary is the sum total of myriad factors including your extensive experience and the country you are currently based in. It may also vary depending on the norms of different airlines. It can range from INR 500,000 to 800,000 per annum.

  Apart from salary, flight attendants receive allowances and bonuses. These comprise in-flight and travel allowances including some extra bonus when you fly during national festivals. Occasionally, you even get paid a part of the profit that the airline makes.
- **Discount on airline tickets** – As a flight attendant, you get a lot of opportunities to travel the world for free and get discounted tickets for your family and friends. Not just this, you can stay at hotels and enjoy your meals at various restaurants at a discount. This means saving up on money and spending it on leisure activities.
- **Wages** – Wages are paid for the 'reserves'. 'Reserves' are periods when you are not on duty but on standby. During this period when you are considered to be on 'reserves', you still get paid for it. Airlines put you on standby so that in case someone reports falling sick or is unable to fly due to unforeseen circumstances,

the persons kept in the 'reserve' can immediately be contacted and asked to report to work. This could happen any moment; even a few hours before the flight is scheduled for takeoff. So, you need to be around and available in case of need. The good news is that you are getting paid for it and you can utilize your day the way you want to. Go shopping, visit your relatives or friends, but make sure you're available in case of an unexpected reserve call.

Pros and Cons

When you are flying, every single flight is different and holds unique experiences. Although it is impossible to share each and every one of them, I would still like to narrate some of my personal experiences that have made flying even more exciting and remarkable for me.

A few years ago, I was operating a flight from Delhi. During our official briefing we were informed that His Holiness The Dalai Lama would be travelling with our airline and would be seated in first class.

When we have very special people on board and especially in first class, we are supposed to respect their privacy. Being a deeply spiritual person, and having read all of the Dalai Lama's quotes, I was itching to get a glimpse of him. To my surprise, after landing, he stayed back on board and expressed his desire to officially meet the crew. All of us gathered to listen to His Holiness, in reverence and in awe.

He met each of us one by one and gave us a piece of paper that had a message which he had written during the flight. With a calming aura and alluring smile, he gave us his blessings. We were bursting with positivity after meeting him.

I have also met many celebrities on board, which is a dream for many. Once we met the team of the Bollywood movie *Simba* and had the absolute pleasure of interacting with the cast. We also took some photos which serve as a reminder of an exciting day.

However, in my long experience of flying, there's one particular incident I will always remember. We had an elderly couple travelling with us, who had come to India for the holidays. During the flight, the husband fell unconscious. I immediately rushed to check his vital signs, and found that he was breathing. Without wasting any time, I called for a medically trained personnel, and inquired about the elderly gentleman's medical history from his wife. We gave him oxygen, and monitored his blood pressure which was running low while the doctor gave him appropriate medical treatment.

After some time, he regained consciousness and was stable. I stayed with this elderly couple for the entirety of the flight and took care of them. When they were leaving, the wife had tears in her eyes and was so thankful to me and rest of the cabin crew members. She gave me their address and invited me to visit them. To this day, I am still in touch with them, and we share a very special bond.

My years as a flight attendant has led me to encounter and experience countless special events which are met with positive feedback from the passengers and ultimately confirmed by the team leader.

If I had to put all the pros in points, it would be as follows:

- **Travel for pleasure** – As a flight attendant, you get to travel around the world, and visit places you never imagined going to before. It's exhilarating to be hopping across the globe and being in two completely different countries in a span of a few hours. It will give you immense pleasure to witness nature's beauty and marvel at human creations.
- **Every day is exciting** – You never have to experience the same day twice. Your work entails handling new challenges, performing each and every responsibility to the best of your capability and making sure you're having fun on board. You also get to travel with different colleagues as per your roster (flight schedule). Every day is exciting and the opportunity to grow is endless.
- **The joy of meeting new people** – You get an opportunity to serve people from all across the globe. This helps you broaden your horizon, and open your mind to diverse worldviews. It

encourages you to learn about different cultures, lifestyles, and personalities. This job offers you ample opportunities to gain knowledge about various places, people, cultures, food, and languages of the world.

Now, the flip side is a different albeit an unpleasant experience. Encountering uncooperative passengers or facing countless unwanted situations is inevitable sometimes. And so, we have to be prepared to handle whatever comes our way.

I cannot forget that first flight of my career where I had to handle an unruly passenger. As soon as he came on board, we noticed that he looked a bit suspicious. When we talked to him, he said he was tired and wanted to sleep. He looked as if he were either drunk or on drugs. The first half of the flight went smoothly. After about 4 hours of flying, he went to the lavatory and smoked a cigarette, which sent us an alert through our smoke detector system. Upon confronting the man, we were met with aggressiveness and unruly behaviour. He hurled obscenities at the cabin crew members. Even the passengers weren't spared.

In a situation like this, as cabin crew, our first step should be to try to de-escalate the situation, which is what my fellow crew was trying to do. But the passenger became even more disorderly, wanted to smoke in the cabin and refused to listen. Finally, a warning was issued stating that if he did not cooperate, he would be detained and handed over to the police upon arrival in Delhi. Nothing calmed him down; he had became a threat to the crew as well as the other passengers.

After giving him several warnings, we had to ultimately handcuff him and force him to remain in his seat until landing (as per the protocol of the airline). He was handed over to the police as soon as we reached Delhi. I still remember all the other passengers clapping for us as if we had caught a criminal. It was a proud moment for us.

I never thought this would happen on my very first flight, I was obviously quite stressed and fearful. Later, I regained my confidence after observing the other senior crew who handled the situation so calmly. This, of course, is the result of years of experience and training. Throughout these years, I too have experienced many such unfavourable situations but time and experience taught me to handle each challenge professionally and fearlessly.

Flight Turbulence

What I am about to share with you is an incident that my colleague went through.

It was a regular flight to Delhi. 40 minutes before landing, the captain announced he was expecting some turbulence as there were heavy thunderstorms around that area. Fortunately, the crew had some time to prepare the cabin for a safe landing whereas in some cases there is no warning and it can be devastating.

Everyone was seated and a friend of mine was sitting in the cabin crew seat at the emergency exit facing the passengers. The wind first hit the plane from the top and there was a sudden drop for a few seconds. What followed was a series of unfortunate events: the passengers were panic-stricken, some of the children suddenly fell sick and started vomitting, the aircraft kept shaking violently while others turned to god for his mercy. Fear struck everyone on that fateful day.

As members of the cabin crew, we're trained to remain calm during severe turbulence, and follow the safety guidelines and procedures to minimise risks. However, in this case, my friend could only make an announcement to request passengers to remain seated with the seat-belt fastened. She was petrified, and felt like she was on an unending roller-coaster ride. The turbulence was so severe she wasn't sure if she'd come out unscathed.

All the passengers were stressed and exhausted after 40 minutes of hell which felt like forever. Later the captain announced that they would be landing in Amritsar as the airport in Delhi was closed due to heavy rain.

Upon reaching Amritsar, everyone let out a sigh of relief. As passengers deboarded the plane, the captain came to see the crew and informed them of how they got lucky to have landed safely. They had almost run out of fuel, and a minute's difference could've turned fatal for all of them. My friend is still haunted by this experience, and it will stay with her for years to come.

The Cons of being a Flight Attendant

No leave or holidays on festivals, birthdays and anniversaries – airlines mostly operate 365 days, so you may have to work on festivals such as Christmas, Holi and Diwali, and also, on personal occasions like birthdays and anniversaries. However, you may plan your schedule in advance and request for leave. The leave is granted mostly on first come first serve basis; the preference is given based on certain factors such as seniority and tenure of job.

- **Odd, long work hours** – You have to work for long and odd hours. One day you have a flight at 2 p.m. and have to work a full 10-hour shift; the very next day, you might have a flight at 5 a.m. that may last just for a few hours. Every day you might have different working hours. Thus, maintaining a routine life and having a regular sleep cycle can be challenging.
- **Jet lag** – Jet lag is extreme tiredness, inability to concentrate and insomnia which manifests itself due to long working hours, lack of sleep, night shifts, and travelling through multiple time zones. It takes time for your body to adjust to your erratic flying schedule and it requires ample self-care and listening to what your body needs to adjust to the routine.
- **Handling emergency situations** – Your job as a flight attendant is unpredictable. You may come across an emergency situation, a disruptive passenger or some technical difficulties. In such situations, you should always stay calm and focus on the complication at hand by applying your knowledge and skills to ensure the safety of your passengers and cabin crew members. It is important to be empathetic, caring and professional while carrying out your responsibilities diligently.
- **Dealing with special passengers** – At times, you might have angry and demanding passengers including some with

disabilities or special needs. In that case, you have to be cognizant of the wishes of those passengers and ensure they're comfortable. When it comes to dealing with unruly passengers, you will have to politely decline their requests if it's disrupting the work of the captain, and in turn, ruining other passengers' in-flight experience. To handle unforeseen situations tactfully, you will receive rigorous training.

I'd like to share a story with you to give you an idea of the kind of situations you may find yourself in. When flying, you'll come face to face with myriad people and unique situations. It's imperative to keep your mind open to all experiences.

A Fortune Teller

We were to fly to Zurich, and the set of crew I was working with on that particular day were some of the most competent and nicest flight attendants I had the pleasure of meeting. The atmosphere was cheerful and plans were made to visit new cities during our layover. I chose to work in business class while my juniors were handling the economy class. Due to a busy schedule, I barely had time to interact with the Indian crew. After my morning service ended, I made my way to them. To my surprise, they looked sullen and extremely upset. At first, they were in denial, but after coaxing the truth out of them, they broke down in front of me.

I was shocked to hear what had happened with them. One of the passengers who claimed to be a fortune teller came to the galley and started a conversation with two of my colleagues. He did not speak to the German crew but targeted only the Indian crew.

He told them something about their past and a few general observations which led them to believe he was an outstanding astrologer who could help them predict their future. Initially, my colleagues had refused to take interest in his generosity, and did not accept his offer. However, he was cunning enough to convince them and came back during the crew's rest time.

He then told them a few things about their past lives and gave them some stones to keep. After his session got over, he demanded

100 dollars as his fees. My colleagues refused to pay him claiming they never asked for his unsolicited prediction in the first place. The man was persistent, and forced them into paying.

I listened to the entire story and asked why they paid him so much and at this, one of my colleagues admitted to feeling hypnotised in his presence. They realised the blunder they had made only when he had left.

I asked them to be confident and go to that passenger and call him in the galley. He quickly came towards us hoping to deceive the rest of the crew members as well. In an authoritative tone, I confronted him, demanding to know why he misled my junior colleagues. I reminded him of his unlawful act, and if there was a repeat of today's events in the future, he would be blacklisted, and barred from flying with us again. I made use of my seniority and years of experience to make sure my juniors weren't duped.

He realised soon enough that he could no longer keep up with the pretence, and had to come clean. He apologised to me and two of my colleagues and handed over the money he had taken without their consent.

My colleagues were so happy and kept thanking me throughout the whole flight. They also got rid of those stones given to them by this so-called fortune teller.

These experiences are part of the airline industry. When we crew members sit together in the lounge during our layovers, we have so much to share; some experiences make us laugh while others are lessons learnt the hard way. But each of our experiences are priceless and unforgettable.

How to Apply

Most of the airlines conduct recruitment drives at regular intervals. They usually advertise on their websites, job portals, and leading newspapers. Be on the lookout for such advertisements. When you find something that works for you, register for the same.

Additionally, you can visit the official websites of leading airlines and check out their career sections for available vacancies. There are also some consultants who are specialists in conducting recruitment drives for leading airlines.

Some Useful Links for Your Reference:

Domestic & International Airlines

https://careers.goindigo.in/Information/careers

https://www.jetairways.com/en/in/careers/careers.aspx

https://www.airvistara.com/trip/careers

http://www.airindia.in/careers.htm

https://www.goteam.in/Candidate/CanHomeBL.aspx

http://www.spicejet.com/careers.aspx

https://www.swiss.com/corporate/EN/careers

https://careers.etihad.com/

https://www.turkishairlines.com/en-in/career/#tcm314-18943

http://careers.qatarairways.com/qatarairways/vacancysearch.aspx

https://www.singaporeair.com/en_UK/in/careers/

Job Portals

https://www.naukri.com/airlines-jobs www.timesjobs.com

www.shine.com www.indeed.com

https://www.monster.com/jobs/q-international-airlines-jobs.aspx

Please follow me on: www.facebook.com/flyhighwithmegha

You can also email me at megha.flyhigh@gmail.com for updates on vacancies related to flight attendant jobs.

All the very best!

Application Process

Applying to airlines might seem daunting but once you understand how to go about it, it becomes a cake walk. In this section, we will cover some key points that will help you get through the application process and empower you to ace the airline interviews.

Cover Letters

A cover letter gives you an opportunity to write about the distinctive qualities you have within a few words. Through a cover letter, you can let the recruiter know about your suitability and seriousness for the job. When writing a cover letter, please avoid writing some common-place sentences such as—I love to travel around the world or I love to serve people.

Try to be a bit different and creative. And don't forget to use the keywords (criteria) described in the advertisement for the position of a flight attendant. Imagine yourself as the hiring manager; what qualities would you like to see in a candidate you are hiring for this job?

The hiring managers need to go through many applications out of which they shortlist only a few who match their standards. Hence, make your cover letter and resume stand out in a positive way. Use an appropriate format, and write the contents under relevant subheadings.

You need to catch the attention of the airline's hiring managers. Follow the KISS principle – *Keep It Short and Simple.*

Explain your achievements in a few words and add examples of your participation in any kind of social service or community work, in case you have done so. You could write about your adventures and show them how spontaneous you are. Let them know you can prove to be an asset to their organisation.

Points to be included in a cover letter

- Place a passport-sized photograph at the top right corner of the cover page.
- Write your correspondence address along with contact details above your photo.
- Write the date on the top left corner.
- Address the letter to the right person using their appropriate title and official name along with their complete postal address. Use Sir/Madam if you don't know their names.
- Write the purpose of your application in the subject line.
- In the next paragraph, mention your qualities and attributes. Explain in brief detail your skills and state why you are the perfect candidate.
- If you are replying to an advertisement, map your qualities according to their requirements.
- State your intentions, and let them know how you can be beneficial to the organisation.
- After you're done writing the cover letter, it's important to end your email in a professional manner. Appropriate email closings include writing 'Yours sincerely' or 'Yours faithfully' at the end followed by your full name below.
- If it's a printed letter, sign above your name.

Example cover letter

75, xyz Lane, Bankhim St.
New Delhi - 110002
Mobile – 605252400
E-mail: megha.flyhigh@gmail.com

14 Oct 2020
Mr Denzil Abraham
Manager – HR
XYZ Airlines International
81, Kingsway Marg, Andheri
Mumbai - 400053

Dear Mr Abraham,

I am applying for the position of a Flight Attendant with reference to your advertisement in *The Career Graph* newspaper dated 8 October 2020.

My extensive experience in customer service with Frontline Global Hotel has taught me the value of providing individualised services to customers. I have been fortunate enough to serve customers of various nationalities and cultures.

The key attributes which make me a competent flight attendant are my customer service skills, effective communication, and sincerity to work to the best of my capabilities. This was recognised last year as I was promoted in my job within the span of a year.

I'm confident in my industrious work ethic and know that my values align with your airline standards. Further, I submit my resume which includes employment history, educational qualifications and contact details.

I look forward to speaking with you or a representative of your organisation in the near future.

Yours sincerely,

Megha Madan

Resume

A resume is a blueprint of your achievements. It maps out your career graph, your ambitions and gives an idea of the kind of candidate you are. It's important to take out time to polish your resume for it to stand out.

Be clear about your objective behind writing a resume. The motive behind presenting a good resume is to get an interview call. That's about it. Nothing more. You want to be called for the interview.

Your resume should showcase your academic credentials, work experience, achievements and your unique qualities.

Interviewers will ask some questions related to information given in your resume, and they expect you to be candid and confident. So, don't write anything that you will not be able to give satisfactory answers for.

Here are a few tips you need to remember while writing a resume:

1. Know what the airline wants. Understand the requirements of each airline well before applying. You must emphasise everything related to customer service including the languages known by you.
2. These days most companies are using the *Applicant Tracking System* (ATS) software that helps hiring executives match the position's job description with candidates, skills and experience. The software uses phrases, themes and keywords to shortlist the best qualified applicants out of hundreds of resumes.

   There are a few keywords which you can pick by going through the job descriptions. For example, if a job description says one must have excellent communication skills, and customer service skills, your resume should address these points using keywords like communication skills, and customer service so that it matches their requirements and can be scanned through ATS.

3. Avoid using text boxes, even when you are submitting your resume online. Create a text only version. Use standard fonts like Cambria, Arial, Helvetica, or Georgia.
4. Use black ink and do not make it colourful. However, you can opt for colours other than black to write the headings.
5. Submit your resume in PDF format. The font size should be 10-12 for the body of the resume and 14-16 for your name. For example, you can use font size 16 for your name, 14 for subheadings like Educational Qualifications, Work Experience, etc., and 12 for the descriptions under subheadings.
6. Use Microsoft Word to write your resume and convert it into a PDF document later. Use margins of at least one inch on all sides.
7. Avoid writing sentences that have been used many times. Try to think outside the box to impress the hiring manager. Your resume should be unique and in accordance with the requirements of the airline. The quality of your resume will determine whether you're selected for the interview round.

Things to be Included in Your Resume

- Full name
- Full address and correspondence address, if different
- E-mail id
- Cellphone number and landline or any alternate number (if available)
- Latest passport-sized professional photo
- Career objective
- Certifications and training
- Employment history (not applicable if you're a fresher)
- Educational qualifications
- Skills and accomplishments
- Interests
- Personal details

- References
- Date and signature

Below is an example of how your resume should look like. Remember to tailor your resume to suit the needs of different airlines.

Megha Madan

235 Af, 9th Avenue, New Delhi -110061

E-mail: megha.flyhigh@gmail.com,

M: 632692154

Objective

Seeking an opportunity to work as a Flight Attendant where I can utilize my skills to create an exquisite aviation experience by providing safety, and great customer service*.

Certificates & Training

- Grooming course from Perfect Makeover Institute
- Certificate in communication skills from MIZU Training
- Certificate in flight attendant training from MIZU Training

Employment History

- Working as a front desk executive with Frontline City Hotel since July 2017

Job Responsibilities:

- Maintaining a pleasing personality and friendly attitude*
- Welcoming and greeting customers at the time of checking in
- Helping customers have a pleasant stay and good check-out experience.

Education

- 12th from Modern Global School, Gwalior, 2015
- Bachelors in Commerce from Jiwaji University, Gwalior, 2018

Skills & Accomplishments

- Won Karate championship at state level in 1995
- Ability to work well in a team
- Ability to establish quick and great rapport with clients

Personal Information

- Age : 22 years
- Height : 165 cm (5'4")
- Nationality : Indian
- Passport : Available
- Interests : Reading books, swimming, interacting with people and participating in community work

Languages known

- English: Advanced
- Hindi: Mother tongue

Date **Megha Madan**

*Keywords which you may find in the job description in the advertisement for hiring flight attendants.

Photograph Guidelines

When applying for a job opening, you definitely need a professional photograph to attach with your resume.

You must check the details of the airline and their requirements for the photograph.

Usually, two types of photos are required – passport size and a full-length photograph (top of your head and your shoes should be visible).

When preparing for getting your photograph clicked, you must follow all the grooming standards and the dress code. Airline recruiters judge a candidate mainly on their appearance, and how confidently they carry themselves. It's essential to make a first strong impression to be eligible for the next round of interviews.

Things to Remember:

1. For airlines, their image is part of a corporate brand. Following strict grooming standards and adhering to uniform guidelines is very important.
2. Airlines insist on their cabin crew to follow a conventional appearance. Female cabin crew should have their hair neatly tied up in a bun or a pony tail. If you have short hair, secure your hair with hair clips to give it a neat and professional look. Male cabin crew members should have a clean, sculpted look. Facial hair is not permitted.
3. You must stand straight with your toes facing forward.
4. You should be in the center of the photograph. In most cases, the airline will instruct you to send the photograph in a particular size. The standard size is 3.5 * 4.5 cm for passport size and 10 * 15 cm for full-length.
5. The background of the photo should be white or plain.
6. You should always have a welcoming smile.
7. Your face should be clearly visible.
8. Do not use photoshop to enhance your photo.
9. Ensure confident and positive body language; avoid putting your hands in your pockets and button your jacket.

Airline Open Days

The day you've been waiting for has finally arrived. To be selected, you must prepare sincerely and exude immense confidence to impress the recruiters.

Before I write anything about the airline open day process of the interview, I would like to add here that the norms vary from airline to airline. Therefore, it is advisable to follow the instructions of the facilitators/HR representatives. The information in this book will make you aware of the various processes that airlines conform to, and help you become well prepared in advance. Keep yourself updated about the latest news and developments in the airline industry by subscribing to relevant journals, newspapers and magazines.

Given below are the interview rounds that you may need to go through on airline open days:

- Meet and greet
- Resume handover
- Group exercises
- Geography, aptitude test
- Personal interview
- Swimming test
- Medical check

Meet and Greet

Remember to reach the venue well in advance in order to give yourself time to freshen up, and touch up your makeup, if required.

More often than not, on airline open days, candidates assemble at the interview premises.

Once you enter the interview premise, you will be observed and judged; so you must come across as confident, well-mannered and presentable right from the beginning. For example, you might enter the lobby of the venue without noticing that one of the interviewers is sitting right across and assessing your behaviour. Thus, do not get busy with your phone or start any unwanted conversation with your fellow candidates. Be conscious of every move you make; even the slightest slip can cost you your dream. The best way is to walk the talk. Behave as if you are a cabin crew member. Sit calmly, greet other interviewers politely, and wait for further instructions. Maintain this image until you walk out of the building.

The Importance of Body Language

Body language is undoubtedly very important; you can win the admiration of the recruiters by making the first interaction count. A lot depends on your first impression, and how you play it to your benefit. Poor body language can ruin your chance even before the interview begins. Regardless of your proficiency and skills, you will find it difficult to change a negative opinion. At this point, all the skills you have won't save you from rejection. However, with the right posture and amicable countenance and behaviour, you can make an impactful impression without uttering a single word.

We communicate not only when we talk but also through non-verbal communication. This is because we are interacting through our body language which includes appearance, facial expressions, how we sit, the way we walk, and how we incorporate the brand image of the airline we're applying to. Let me ask you a question: have you ever formed an opinion about someone you don't know, by just looking at him or her? I am sure we all have. That's basic human nature. We form opinions during the very first interaction.

In the same fashion, from the moment you walk into the venue, your interview has started. Everybody around you is in some way judging you. Even before you greet the interviewers, they have formed an opinion in a matter seconds just by looking at you. Right from how you dress to your body language to how you carry yourself will stand as a visual representation of who you are.

Remember the old saying, *'The first impression is the last impression'.* This still holds true.

And don't forget there will be hundreds of other participants that the interviewers have to screen. How much time do you think they would invest on each participant considering they have to select only a handful out of hundreds of applications? Hardly two minutes. They will be very picky about who they choose, and a small issue in terms of your body language can prove to be a setback.

Coming back to being well prepared, a good way to ensure confidence on D-day is by rehearsing at home before the open day. Self-assess and improvise. Check the problem areas and fix them. Practice in front of the mirror or record your video. Enact the interview at home multiple times. Wear your dress and practice to walk with confidence.

This is your best chance so give it all you have.

Now let's talk about some aspects of body language.

Eye Contact

A person failing to maintain eye contact is perceived as insecure or underconfident. When you are in front of the interviewer and not able to maintain good eye contact, you might not be able to establish a good rapport with him/her. If you are a fresher and attending an interview for the first time, it may be a challenge to keep the right balance; however, practice will help make you get better.

Eye contact requires maintaining a balance. This means avoiding looking down when a question is asked, but it doesn't mean staring constantly at the interviewer either! Answering confidently by looking directly at the interviewer and looking calm and composed are the keys to a good interview. Avoid moving your legs often and too many hand movements. Otherwise, you'll end up giving the impression of being nervous and under-prepared.

If there is more than one interviewer in the panel, you can focus your gaze on one interviewer for a few seconds, then shift to the next and so on. Try to not just answer to the person who asked you the question. Remember it's a group question for which all the interviewers would like to know the answer.

If you are asked a question which needs some thinking, it is okay to look up, and nod, and take your time before answering the question.

Smile

What attracts you when you look at the pictures of cabin crew? In fact, what do you notice when you look at an airline advertisment? A pleasant face with a bright smile. A genuine smile can make other people register a good impression about you in their minds.

Cabin crew would also like to be accompanied by smiling passengers on board. It makes the environment vibrant and lively.

When going for an interview you must always sport a happy disposition. Not only will you feel instantly cheerful but you will also let go of all your nervousness and stress.

Handshake

Perfecting the skill of a proper handshake makes for a great first impression. A handshake should be firm and not weak. You should apply a normal grip while holding someone's hand. A weak handshake conveys underconfidence and shows you are nervous or in a hurry. A firm handshake gives a good impression. You should stand straight with your thumb up. Two to three pumps of handshaking is considered ideal.

Always use a good hand cream to ensure your hands are soft. If you have sweaty palms, wipe them with a clean tissue or handkerchief and then initiate the handshake.

In the briefing where we meet all the other crew members, we introduce ourselves and then shake hands. Every individual has a distinct style and after every handshake we make an impression in our mind about that person at that very moment. I remember one flight crew member who used to almost crush our hands! Everyone would be hesitant to extend their hand whenever he would arrive. We used to jokingly call him 'bone-crusher'!

A firm handshake means a consistent grip while applying balanced pressure all over the hand and not only on the fingers or thumb.

Once you are through with the meet and greet, you will be called for the next round.

General Appearance

In this round they will verify the information regarding your height and weight given by you in your resume, and check if they match with their ariline standards. You will be asked to stand straight in order to measure your height. Your face would be required to face the wall and you will be asked to raise your hands beside the measuring scale to check your arm reach. This will be followed by a weight check. Your weight should be in proportion to your height. You must know your BMI, which you would have mentioned in your resume, and the numbers should match at the time of screening.

In some airlines, they also check your skin for any visible scars, acne, tattoos or medical conditions. I would suggest that if you have any scars which can be concealed with the help of makeup, then you may go ahead and do so. There is no hard and fast rule for what is acceptable and what is not.

If any scar or mole is affecting your appearance, there is a possibility that the airline might have an issue with it. It's important to understand that flawless skin is an unreal beauty standard. Don't let it dishearten you from giving your best shot. Many of my friends who don't have 'ideal' skin conditions are successfully working in the airline industry. Here's where makeup comes to the rescue. Learn the art of makeup and you'll be good to go.

After you have successfully cleared this round, your name will be announced for the next round.

Resume Handover

In case of a walk-in interview, the assessor may decide to take your resume at the very beginning of the interview. In other cases, the airline might ask you to first fill up an online application form. Upon selecting your profile they will call you for the interview.

It is important to ensure that all the information is complete and filled accurately in the application form. You will be competing with hundreds of like-minded applicants who have done their share of work, and are on a mission to get selected. If your interviewers find out something which does not adhere to their airline requirements, your chances of getting selected are next to none.

Most airlines will ask you to gather in a group first and hand over your resume. Following this, the screening process will begin. You have to be vigilant at all times and keep your eyes and ears open. In the introduction session the HR team will also introduce themselves and this is your opportunity to remember the names of the panel.

When you meet them again for the interview round and greet them by using their names, you set a precedent for how the rest of the interview will unfold. Being attentive helps you analyse the situation and prepare yourself accordingly. The recruiters will thus form a positive impression of you.

When called for a self-introduction, most candidates give answers which are generic. For instance:

'Hello, I am Sunita. I am 22 years old. I have finished my graduation in commerce from Jiwaji University. As far as my strength is concerned, I am very hard-working and passionate. I want to become a flight attendant because I love to travel across the world and meet people from various backgrounds.'

Doesn't it sound as though she has learned it by heart and seems like a very basic answer? Now let's consider another approach:

'Hello, I am Sunita. I am 22 years old. I have completed my graduation in commerce. I was one of the best badminton players in my college. My winning attitude has always kept me ahead in life. I work very well independently or as part of a team. I am an avid team player and goal-oriented. I was fortunate enough to travel to Sri Lanka with my family last year where I could experience Sri Lankan culture and food. I would love to work as a flight attendant where I could employ my natural talents and skills. At the same time, I can explore the world.'

Based on the above sample, you can write your own introduction and put your creative skills at work. Make it interesting but relevant. As mentioned earlier, practice self-introduction in front of the mirror, record it and play it back. See how it sounds to you. Evaluate it and keep working on it till its perfect. To put your creative skills at test, give your introduction in front of your family and friends to better understand how it sounds. This will help you identify the problem areas.

Always remember that when the interviewer is asking you common questions, you are being observed constantly. As soon as you walk into that room, your screening begins. Airlines require a cabin crew member to have impeccable grooming standards, positive body language, and a cheerful attitude. You will constantly be judged on these attributes, so remember to present yourself accordingly.

Once you are through with the first round, the interviewer may inform you if the selected candidates will get a call or an email within a few days for the next round of interview. And if the next level of interview is happening on the same day, the shortlisted candidates will have to wait outside and the rest will be asked to leave.

Group Exercises

Group discussion exercises and presentations are primarily designed to focus on your behavioral and communication skills. You will be thoroughly evaluated on the following skills: team work, initiative-taking abilities, confidence, communication and influencing skills.

During the group exercises, candidates will be split into groups of 8-10 people. There are mainly three types of exercises.

1. **Introductions to the group:** The interviewer may ask you to introduce yourself to both the group and the facilitators. You may also be asked some short questions, such as why you want to work as a flight attendant. Mind you, this is a golden opportunity to show your unique caliber although this can be nerve-wracking. In order to ensure your speech is fluent and eloquent, rehearse your introduction in front of the mirror as many times as you can. Remember, practice makes perfect. To test yourself further, come up with creative questions you think the recruiter might ask. Prepare those in advance if you want to proceed to the next round.

   Never forget, this is your chance to shine in front of the interviewers so that you have a higher chance of getting hired. Hence, write your introduction, prepare for other possible questions and rehearse. (For a guide on self-introduction, please refer to question number 1 in the chapter titled 'Interview Questions'.)

   Another form of introduction is **fact-finding**. You may be given the task to introduce yourself to the person next to you and find out some information or interesting facts about them in return. For example, who they are, what they do, what is their most memorable moment and the likes. To make your interaction more fulfilling you can also ask them questions about their childhood days, schooling, role models, family background or hometown. The idea is to squeeze out as much information as possible within a given time frame.

   By probing you can help that person reveal some interesting facts in front of you. This will make you come up as a leader and highlight your leadership qualities in front of the HR.

2. **Extempore:** You may then be asked to speak on a topic for a minute or two. Or you will be shown a picture

about which you'll be asked to talk about. This is called extempore. Topics are usually general in nature.

Listed below are some topics that will give you a fair idea on how to prepare for an airline interview:

i. Who is your favorite actor and why?
ii. What change would you bring to the world if given a chance?
iii. Love marriage vs. arranged marriage – what would you prefer?
iv. Social media is killing creativity. Yes or no?
v. Digital payments are secured and is India ready to become a cashless economy?
vi. Hard work or smart work?
vii. Soft skills matter more than technical skills. Do you agree or disagree?
viii. Should Hindi be a mandatory language in India?

The above questions are illustrative. During a group discussion, questions are asked on current affairs, social issues, questions of general interest, education, business, politics, and sports. Therefore, you must make it a habit to subscribe to news apps to get the crux of what is happening around you.

Remember: Speaking too much does not guarantee your selection for the next round. You're being held upto the highest standards and the interviewer is observing you in multiple aspects such as communication skills, listening to others, respecting the views of others, presenting your views and ideas. Believe in quality more than quantity; this will ensure your selection for the next round.

The takeaway here is that you are competing with thousands of candidates. Out of those candidates, only a few will be able to make it to the end and be offered a job. So, imagine what level of preparation you are required to do to get through this dream job of yours.

3. **Group presentation:** You will be given an object such as a pen or paper clip and asked to sell it to the group or speak about it for two minutes. Alternatively, you may be given a picture and asked to sell it as a new holiday destination to the group. Cabin crew members are required to possess excellent persuasion skills to sell some products in the flight; hence, perfecting selling skills is a must for this job.

   Master tip: To answer such questions, you need to focus on WH questions. Suppose you are to speak on a paper clip. Prepare yourself around WH questions, such as: What is the importance of a paper clip? What types of paper clips are available? What was your last experience with a paper clip?

   By using WH questions, you will be able to handle any question directed at you. You have to repeat these questions in your head, and make a mental note of possible points you can make. If given a chance to write down the answers, make bullet points using only the key words. For instance, you can write something about paper clips as hints—

   - Holds a bunch of paper together
   - Saves time
   - Chronological manner
   - Assists in making paper ready for an interview

   This excercise will help you recall things faster and enable you to show your speaking skills.

   Let's try and elaborate on the usage of a paper clip as part of your two-minute speech: 'A paper clip is very helpful. It helps hold together a bunch of paper. It saves time when we can clip the papers in a chronological order'… and so on. Now describe your experience with the paper clip: 'The last time I used it was when I was collecting all the papers for my interview. I tucked my resume, photographs, and other documents into the paper clip. It is truly a life saver.' Though this speech will not last for 2 minutes, this is for you to understand how you can approach a topic when asked to speak.

Going down memory lane, when I was given a picture to speak about at my interview, I had looked at it for a couple of seconds and had spoken on it for nearly 2 minutes. Some of us were able to do that but a few candidates were not even able to speak for 30 seconds. That is primarily because they hadn't practiced enough.

Practice is what makes you perfect. So, try using WH questions as tools but do not limit yourself. Start making notes, and practice speaking in front of the mirror. I used to record my own voice and listen to it several times. If I committed any mistake, I had a chance to rectify it the next time. Speak for at least 3 minutes on any topic and practice multiple times.

Here's a detailed look at all the qualities that airlines predominantly look for during group interviews:

- **Initiative skills**: How well can a candidate initiate the discussion. Let's suppose the topic is: love marriage vs arranged marriage. What would you prefer?

  You can start speaking on the topic by saying – 'Hello/ Good morning, everybody. I am Megha Madan. First of all, I would like to thank each of you for being part of this discussion. If given a chance, I would prefer… because... (and then you can give reasons to support your choice as to why you would prefer love marriage or arranged marriage).
- **Communication skills**: Are you able to convey your ideas clearly? Do you allow the other fellow members to speak? Do you listen to them attentively? Are you a good listener?

  If your answer is 'Yes' to the above questions, then you are a good communicator. As a flight attendant, you come across people from various backgrounds with different nationalities. It is a must that you should not only have great speaking skills but also possess excellent listening skills.

- **Teamwork**: Do you co-operate and facilitate in a team? Do you agree to disagree using your soft skills? The purpose of a group discussion is not merely to show how much one can speak and exhibit one's knowledge, but also how well one can accommodate the other participants and let them speak when they have a point.
- **Selling skills**: In almost every airline, it is mandatory to sell duty free products or eatables (in low cost airlines) to the passengers. You shouldn't be surprised to hear that there is some target assigned to sell the products. However, the good news is that this is also an opportunity to earn a few extra bucks in the form of incentives. So, your selling skills will also be evaluated during the interview. It doesn't mean that you have to be a professional sales person to get through this section. However, they will observe your persuasion and presentation skills.

  When you are given a chance to sell a product, just think of why you would buy that as a customer. Think of two or three positive points about that product and present that in front of the hiring managers, as if they are your real clients. You may also like to emphasise on the value the products offer; such as enhancing one's personality, or make one's life comfortable. You are required to put your creativity at work to excel in this test. But rest assured, nothing is rocket science. With better guidance and practice, you will be able to polish your skills.
- **Leadership skills**: Airlines want a person who knows how to take charge. So in case you don't get the chance to speak up during the group discussion, try to grab the opportunity to conclude the topic. Reiterate the points

others have mentioned into a cohesive structure, and give your parting thoughts about the topic.

Airlines prefer people who possess leadership skills. The job of a flight attendant is not limited to just customer service but extends to other qualities too, especially leadership skills. There are many circumstances where flight attendants are required to motivate other team members, hold each other's hands, stay calm, take the right decision during an emergency and encourage others to perform their duties to work as a team to achieve a single goal.

There are a few points you need to keep in mind when you attend a group exercise:

1. Greet every participant.
2. Focus on the quality of the content. Avoid repetition or long sentences.
3. Maintain your calm. Don't get aggressive.
4. Put your point across when you get an opportunity. Do not argue.
5. Influence others with logical answers. Do not try to force your opinion on others.
6. Don't interrupt other participants while they are engaged in discussion. When you have a point, raise your hand and wait for your turn.
7. Maintain a pleasant countenance throughout the group discussion.
8. Don't sit idle. Show your active participation and put your points across.
9. Handle criticism diplomatically. Acknowledge it first and then make your point strategically.
10. Split your presentation into three parts: introduction, body and conclusion.

Problem Solving as a Group

This is one of my favourite activities to do as a group. Problem-solving is an opportunity to show your ability to participate well in a team, leadership skills, friendliness and co-operation with other participants. It will also help show how good you are at following instructions and voicing your opinion in front of the group in an assertive manner.

In this group exercise, you will be assigned a task as a group and asked to solve a problem within a stipulated time frame. The facilitators will play no role and you will be observed from a distance by them. They will be taking note of your overall behavior within a team setting.

The outcome doesn't really matter in this section. No one is declared a winner. So, relax. What matters the most in this activity is how well you perform in all aspects. Always show your willingness and enthusiasm. Agree to disagree but do not display a negative attitude. Show that you believe in finding solutions to every problem. If you have to disagree, do it politely while putting across your point of view.

An Example of a Team-Work Task

1. Each participant is given 10 paper shapes.
2. Their aim is to construct an image.
3. To construct an image from 10 different paper shapes, each participant needs to swap shapes and co-operate with each other.
4. The group is given 10 minutes to complete the task.

Examples of Positive Behaviour

- Show co-operation and support the group members to construct the object (e.g., an elephant) using interpersonal skills.
- Demonstrate leadership skills and allow others to participate. Do not try to dominate others.

- Put your point of view across politely yet firmly.
- Do not be adamant about accepting multiple view points.
- Ask for input from other group members.
- Participate in and help facilitate discussions.
- Most importantly, enjoy the task.
- Show enthusiasm.
- Always wear a cheerful smile on your face.

Role Play

Oh gosh! I heaved a sigh of relief after finishing this task. For some of you who are not really into acting or theatre, this task can prove to be intimidating. But remember that you will not be judged upon your acting skills; rather you will be observed on how efficiently you handle tasks and how you maintain your attitude. So, it's all about never giving up and believing 'the customer is the king'.

For this task, you will be handed a sheet with some briefing on it. Normally, you will get a minute to prepare for it. Once you have done your preparation, an assessor will act as your customer. The situation is surely challenging but here are a few tips you can keep in mind:

- Listen to the customer's complaint carefully.
- Acknowledge the issue by using some key phrases such as: 'I understand, Mr/Miss__________, I can see that Mr/Miss__________'
- Provide solutions such as: 'I understand that Mr/Miss_____ and that's why we are doing __________ for you.'
- Stay calm even if the customer raises his/her voice.
- Hear the customer out. Do not cut him/her off.
- See what you can offer the customer as freebies within your capacity, if required.
- Most importantly, do not give up unless you have provided a solution to the customer.

Geography, Aptitude Test and English (written test)

Geography

Domestic airlines operating in India may not conduct geographical knowledge tests. However, they may ask you about different locations of airports situated in India. Also, they may ask general knowledge questions like what is Jaipur famous for.

When applying for international airlines, you may anticipate being asked questions related to global geography. Let's assume that you are an interviewer from a Singapore-based airline. The following are a few points the candidates must keep in mind:

- Names of different destinations in the world that this particular airline covers.
- Names of famous airports and their locations.
- Names of different airports in Singapore.
- Famous monuments and their locations in Singapore or maybe in the world.
- The capital of the country and specialty of that place.
- What Singapore is famous for.

During my interview, I was asked the following questions:

- What is the capital of Switzerland?
- What is Switzerland famous for?
- What is the official language of Switzerland?
- What is the full form of ICAO & IATA?

Normally, there are multiple choices for each question. However, you can also expect a few questions related to global geography during the interview.

Aptitude Test

Airlines rarely conduct aptitude tests but I want you to be prepared for everything.

Knowledge of basic mathematics will work to your advantage and help you get through this test. Start practicing elementary math, develop reasoning ability and hone your problem-solving skills to ace the exam.

Sample Aptitude Questions:

1. An airplane covers a certain distance at a speed of 240 kmph in 5 hours. At what speed it must travel to cover the same distance in 1 hour?

   (A) 300 kmph (B) 600 kmph
   (C) 720 kmph (D) 1200 kmph

   [Hint: Distance = speed * time]

2. 9 girls and 12 boys complete a task in 12 days. 12 girls and 12 boys finish it in 10 days. How many days will it take for 10 girls and 10 boys to finish the task?

   (A) 8 days (B) 10 days
   (C) 12 days (D) None of these

3. The cost price of 15 bananas is equal to the selling price of 12 bananas. Find the profit or loss percentage.

   (A) 15% (B) 25%
   (C) 35% (D) 45%

4. The usual price of a bouquet is USD180. On Christmas, they offer a 15% discount. Calculate the cost of the bouquet on Christmas.

   (A) 143 (B) 148
   (C) 153 (D) 158

5. The cost of a watch is INR 36500. The tax charged is 8%. Calculate the bill amount.

   (A) 38430 (B) 39430
   (C) 39420 (D) 36400

The above questions are examples of the type of questions that can appear in the aptitude test. I have taken one question each from different chapters in Mathematics such as Time & Work, Percentage, Average, and Partnership. To clear this test, search for your high school math textbooks and brush up on your number game. Usually, domestic airlines do not have such aptitude tests. So, even if you're not good at Mathematics, you can still apply and stand a chance to get the job. However, do check the format of the entire interview process to confirm if the airline you are applying to has such a test or not.

English Test

The English test is mandatory for all the airlines. You will be evaluated on four different sets of skills in the English language: Listening, reading, writing, and speaking. Thus, it is of utmost importance to develop your English skills.

A flight attendant has to communicate with passengers from diverse backgrounds such as English-speaking passengers with different dialects such as British, American, Australian, and also non-English speaking passengers who don't speak English as their first language. No matter what the background of the passengers may be, cabin crew must always be able to communicate clearly and handle situations well.

Let me share with you my experience of learning English.

I studied in a school where Hindi was the primary language. Way back in the 1990s when I was in school, English medium schools did not exist in my home town. People who could speak English were considered superior and be looked at with wonder and respect.

I used to think that speaking fluent English was not my cup of tea. When I completed my higher secondary, my desire to become a flight attendant was intense. I realised then the importance of learning and speaking fluent English.

Not knowing how to speak fluent English was the roadblock in all the dreams about my goals. I was haunted by it everyday, and felt scared and helpless. But then, I had two choices. Either I give up on my dream due to lack of mastery over English or learn it the hard way. I chose the latter. I decided to not only learn English, but to be the best at it.

To start with, I joined an institute to learn spoken English which was located near my house in Shivpuri, MP. With consistent efforts I became good at spoken English within a few months. However, this was not sufficient. My goal was to become excellent in English. That's when I decided to push myself and inculcated habits to become a confident speaker and writer of the English language.

I began by putting in 4-6 hours of studying hard. I used to read newspapers and story books aloud. I would practice in front of the mirror, translate Hindi songs into English and sing them just to have fun. In those days, smartphones didn't exist, which meant I had no access to platforms like YouTube. So, I resorted to watching English movies on the television.

I memorised more than 3000 high usage words from a dictionary. Those were words I had collected from stories, dialogues and anecdotes. Did you know that even a fluent speaker of English language does not use more than 3000 words in a day? As you would have already noticed, most words used during a conversation or a speech get repeated. Only the form of words changes such as Base form, Past Simple, and Past Participle.

Slowly, I also started gaining confidence in speaking situational and profession-based sentences. Have you noticed any Bollywood actor or a sports person, who was not very good at English initially, starting to speak fluent English in front of the media a few months later? This happens because they learn specific words and sentences related to their profession. I call them short sentences or short dialogues.

Let's look at some short dialogues to get a clearer idea.

Self-introduction

- Hi, I am Tina Singh.
- I completed my graduation in commerce from Delhi University.
- I have been a bright student throughout and have won many awards.
- I was the winner of a debate competition at my school.

- I am a quick learner and possess great communication skills.
- I accept challenges and do not give up until I finish the task.

Flight-related Sentences

- Can I see your boarding pass, please?
- We are ready for takeoff. Please fasten your seat belt.
- Allow me to show you the meal selection for today.
- How would you like to pay?
- I'm afraid we have no other seat available.
- If the situation doesn't get better, I will call for a medically qualified personnel.
- I would like you to kindly pay attention to our safety video.
- Look forward to seeing you again soon. Hope you had a great flight.

The above sentences have been given for guidance. Based on these examples, you can develop your own stock of words and sentences that can be used timely. However, intense practice is required when it comes to speaking fluent English. You may become good in writing and reading by studying the language but unless you practice speaking English aloud and learn to pronounce each word correctly, it is next to impossible to speak fluent English with confidence.

Practical Ways to Improve Your English

- Read children's story books ALOUD. Become the characters written in the book and talk to yourself as if you are portraying the roles of each character.
- Listen to English songs.
- Watch YouTube videos to enhance your English skills.
- Record your own voice and listen to it.

  Tip: *Speak about your daily routine in English: What you did the entire day, what are you planning for today? How was your day yesterday? What happened last weekend? What are your future plans?*

- Join any good institute and learn English. It will prove to be a smart investment of your time and money.
- Spend quality time trying to improve your English. Take it very seriously.

Remember, no matter how good-looking and smart you are, without mastering English, becoming a flight attendant will remain a dream and not translate into reality.

Now let's take a look at the format of the English test during the assessment. If you are aware of IELTS (International English Language Testing System), you can skip reading further about the English testing format because this is more or less similar to the IELTS pattern.

Reading

This entails a comprehension test in which you will be given several passages of 600-700 words followed by a few questions. The answers to the questions are already embedded in the text provided. After reading the passage, you will be asked about the main ideas, vocabulary, details, inferences, etc. You will have to complete writing the answers within a certain time frame.

Writing

The writing section comprises independent and integrated tasks. For the independent task, you will be asked to write an essay that explains and supports your ideas on an issue. The integrated task will require you to read and then write a summary that throws light on the significant points from the text and how they connect to the passage.

For instance:

Think about a bad experience you have encountered.

- What happened? Did you expect it?
- What was your response? How did you handle it?
- What did you do to overcome the situation?

English Grammar

When I had to learn grammar, I referred to Wren and Martin's *High School Grammar and Composition*. I found this book quite useful. But you can refer to any good high-school level English grammar book.

Sample Questions

Choose the correct options from *who, which, whose*:

- This is the bank was robbed yesterday.
- He is Shyam sister works in my office was present there at that time.
- This is the boy hit me on my nose.

Supply appropriate comparative or superlative degree to each of the following:

- Delhi is (the coldest/colder) than any other city.
- He can speak (better/the best) English than anybody else here in this office.

Put the verbs into the correct form (past perfect tense):

- I (reach) the station after the train (leaves)
- I could not remember the poem that I (learn) a week ago.

Choose the appropriate options to complete the sentences:

- These electronic items______bought for daily use so you______ have a comfortable stay.
  - were/can
  - have been/can
  - was/might
  - has been/may

Speaking

There are two types of tasks in the speaking section: independent and integrated. For independent tasks, speakers are assessed on their ability to answer opinion questions on subjects they are acquainted with. In the integrated tasks, you are supposed to read a short passage, listen to a conversation on the same topic, then answer a question that needs you to combine the information from the text and the conversation. The candidate may take notes and then refer back to those notes before giving their answers.

Always remember that right from the resume submitting stage to the group exercises to the personal interview, your English speaking skills will be assessed.

Listening

From an airline's interview perspective, your listening skills are evaluated starting from your interaction with the interviewers and the applicants. When you submit your resume, you may be asked a few general questions. When you participate in group exercises, you are required to listen to the other participants carefully so that you can respond accordingly.

As a flight attendant, you get to interact with lots of people of different nationalities including those whose native language is not English. So, it becomes imperative to ensure your listening skills are up to the mark so that you can handle the customer's queries effectively.

Personal Interview

The personal interview or one-on-one interview is designed to check your suitability for the position. The hiring managers will check your skills by asking behavioural questions that also include negative style questions. They will use S-T-A-R questions. Your answer to these questions will help them understand how you would react in similar situations. Through the personal interview, they would assess your decision-making skills, promptness, confidence, problem-solving skills, communication and persuasion skills.

A set of questions are asked to evaluate your skills. You are also free to ask questions in case you do not understand certain things. From attire to body language to tonality to sentence formation to overall presentation—everything matters during the personal interview.

However, the most important thing you need to keep in mind is that it is a conversation and not a monologue. So, enjoy answering the questions, be friendly but maintain a professional approach. I have listed some interview questions with strategic answers in this book which can help you crack the personal interview.

I have covered more than 50 frequently asked questions and also some situation-based questions in the chapter 'Questions and Strategic Answers'.

Announcement Reading Round

An extremely vital part of a flight are the announcements. The flight starts with an announcement and ends with one.

The entire flight will have various announcements from welcome to before and after takeoff to calmly assuring passengers during extreme turbulence or delay to flight landing and farewell. Therefore, you must familiarise yourself with different variations of the announcements.

As far as announcements go, the interviewer will judge you on the following aspects:

1. Clarity of speech.
2. Voice modulation
3. Intonation and pronunciation

This sounds like an easy task. However when you are given a script, it is not as easy as it sounds. You may also need to practice reading Hindi passages.

On international airlines operating from India, flight attendants are required to do Hindi announcements for their Hindi speaking passengers on board.

Listening to your own voice in the cabin is an enjoyable experience.

Swimming Test

All the international airlines conduct swimming tests. Clearing this test is one of the most important requirements to become a flight attendant. Failure to pass the swimming test will nullify any chance you have even if you possess other excellent skills.

Some international airlines prefer to take the swimming test in the preliminary round to filter candidates.

Take your swimming lessons seriously. Practice as hard as you can. You will be asked to swim a lap or two, unsupervised.

Medical Test

Once you have successfully cleared all the above rounds, you will be given a date and information about the place where you need to go for a complete body checkup.

You will be given a form where you will be required to declare your complete medical history, and inform the doctor about any prevailing conditions or previous surgeries. Do not be dishonest; fill out every bit of information with utmost sincerity.

The medical test will consist of blood tests, urine tests, a height and weight check, ears and eyes test, x-ray, ultrasound and a few more compulsory tests. This is to determine whether you are completely healthy to take the responsibility of such a challenging job.

The STAR Technique

STAR stands for Situation, Task, Action, and Result. The interviewer will ask you some general questions and use the STAR technique to evaluate your answers.

Knowing how this works would work to your advantage and will open the door to your dream job.

Here are some examples of STAR questions:

- Tell us about a time when you were not supported by your boss and how you handled it.
- What was the most difficult situation you handled in your life? How did you manage it?

The best way to answer a STAR question is to answer it with a story from your personal experience. Do not beat around the bush. Take 40 seconds to 1 minute to explain your answer and try to cover all the four parameters, i.e., Situation, Task, Action, and Result.

Interview Questions with Strategic Answers

During the personal interview, the interviewers will ask you questions that focus on your previous experiences. However, to start with, you may be asked something related to your educational background, work experience, or why you want to become a flight attendant to break the ice. To help you learn more about different styles of questions, I have listed some frequently asked questions as examples. I have also included strategic answers in order to help you get a better idea, be able to anticipate, and prepare well in advance to ace your cabin crew interview.

It is natural to feel nervous during the interview; I had felt the same anxiety and nervousness. But that's the beauty of it all; this experience will be a key takeaway to understand and learn how to manage your emotions and stay calm in the face of it all. That's what the recruiters are looking for.

That's what this job demands from you.

Now, let's look at some sample questions and their answers:

Ice-Breaker Questions:

- **Tell me something about yourself.**

This can be used to start a group discussion or during the final round of interview as an introductory question. Some people think it's not a big deal to give a self-introduction and it doesn't require any preparation. However, let me tell you this is a trick question, and is part of the elimination round.

Interviewers ask you this question to make you comfortable. At the same time, they would like to know your strengths and qualities. The smart way to handle this question would be based on the situation in which it is asked, so answer accordingly. Highlight the key points that distinguish you from the rest and make you the right fit for the position of a flight attendant.

During the group activity, the facilitator will ask you to include the following information in your introduction:

- **Your name**
- **Age**
- **City**
- **An interesting fact about you**
- **Why you want to be a flight attendant**

To tell them an interesting fact and why you want to be a flight attendant, highlight some of the skills that make you a perfect candidate for this job. Also, talk about any voluntary work you have done or if you have an adventurous spirit.

Strategic answer:

'Good morning, everyone, I am Smita Singh. I am 22 years old and I come from the vibrant city of Jaipur which is also known as the Pink City. When I was 10 years old, I got a chance to travel by air. That's when I saw some people serving passengers with a big smiles on their faces. Out of curiosity when I asked my mother who they were, she told me they were cabin crew members. A cabin crew member came to me and offered a glass of juice with a lovely smile on her face and talked to me for a few seconds. That memory is still etched in my mind. I knew then that I wanted to become a flight attendant and serve people so that they leave with a genuine smile and a beautiful memory to take back home.'

If this question is asked during the final interview, then you do not need to talk about age and family background unless asked. The hiring managers are mainly interested in knowing whether your qualities and skills are a perfect match for the cabin crew position. They're keen on confirming whether you are efficient and professional in your attitude. Thus, while answering this question, consider including your educational qualifications, work experience and skills.

Here are a few key points you should remember when asked about your interest in becoming a flight attendant:

- Greet the interviewers.
- Mention your qualifications.
- Add some interesting facts about you from your school/college days such as your academic capabilities or achievements in sports.
- Talk about your strengths.

Tip: Your introduction should be approximately 90 seconds.

Remember: *Be sure about your body language. Maintain eye contact with the interviewers even when they are not looking at you. That would show that you are confident and well-prepared. Sit or stand in an upright position, do not move your hands too frequently. Non-verbal communication is equally important.*

Strategic answer (for final interview):

'Good morning, everyone, I graduated in commerce from X college. I have 2 years of work experience as a customer care representative at XYZ company. I went the extra mile to resolve every customer's problem. I have always believed that excellent customer service is as important for personal growth and satisfaction as it is for the growth of a company. I have been an avid team player and know how to use my strong leadership skills whenever the situation requires it.'

Your answer:

____

____

____

____

____

____

____

____

____

____

- **Why do you want to want to become a flight attendant?**

Highlight some of your highly praised characteristics and interesting facts about your personality which make you a perfect, sought-after candidate for this unique position. You can also express how fascinating this job is to you, the kind of responsibilities it entails and how well-prepared you are to take it up. Further, mention the efforts you have put in to acquire these skills. Share a story from your previous job to validate your points.

Strategic answer for candidates with previous job experience:

'I want to become a cabin crew member with ________ airlines (name of the airline you are giving the interview for) because this would give me ample opportunities to interact with a diverse set of people and serve their needs using my interpersonal skills. I want to be part of an industry that will challenge me every day and give me a chance to travel to different parts of the country/world. In my last job, I was part of a large group and that's where I learnt about team spirit. I was a great team player there and always fulfilled my responsibilities in the best possible way and further encouraged my team to always keep the spirits high.'

Strategic answers for freshers:

'I want to become a flight attendant because (name of the airline you are giving the interview for) has a great reputation. To grow mutually, I can utilize my communication skills and passion for delivering exceptional customer service that will create a memorable experience for the passengers.'

You can also add:

'This job would present me with many opportunities to provide life-saving service to different passengers. At the same time, I would get to see the world, experience different cultures, and meet people from all walks of life.

'There's no better way of living than to get to fly across the globe and live my dream while serving people.'

P.S. The above is an illustrative answer provided only to guide you. Please do not use the very same words. To remain authentic, modify your answer to suit your personality and situation and give it your personal touch.

Your answer:

Based on the above answer, write your answer in your own words:

____

____

____

____

____

____

____

____

____

- **What is your daily routine?**

  OR

  How do you spend your time?

Say something which adds value to your profile. You can talk about how you've prepared for this job. Mention that you like reading motivational books, and also love to keep your self up to date with the happenings of the world with the help of newspapers and journals. You can also mention the physical activities you do to keep yourself fit and healthy.

Strategic answer:

'I am an early riser. I believe in keeping myself fit. So I do some exercise such as cycling, and jogging. After my workout, I ensure I eat a healthy meal for breakfast. I plan my day ahead, and proceed towards the tasks. To stay on top of the news, I read several articles on the airline industry as well as on current affairs.'

Your answer:

- **What are your hobbies?**

They may ask you several questions related to your hobbies. If you are making it up to sound smart, be careful and be prepared to answer some cross questions related to that. If you have travelled to many parts of the country, you can say that your hobby is travelling and learning about diverse cultures, food, and places. If you are a social person, you can say that your hobby is interacting with people. These are the hobbies which are required for a cabin crew position.

Strategic answer:

'Although my hobbies range from reading to cycling, I feel more connected when I interact and socialise with people from diverse backgrounds. It is thrilling to explore and understand myriad traditions and cultures. It fills me with immense pride to live in a country like ours which is a nucleas for cultural diversity.'

Your answer:

____

____

____

____

____

____

____

____

____

- **What do your friends or colleagues say about you?**

This is again a question related to your strengths and weaknesses. Answer it carefully. What you end up saying about your strengths and weaknesses should turn out to be a valuable resource for them. Therefore, do not give a generic answer.

Talk about those strengths which are highly appropriate for this job such as communication skills, team work, problem-solving skills, and customer service. Try and give an example and share experiences from your previous job.

Strategic answer:

'I have great problem-solving skills. I am a friend in need. My friends and colleagues know that they can always rely on me to come up with possible solutions in a difficult situation. Apart from that, I am a great team player and a quick and enthusiastic learner. I have also got a customer service excellence award at my previous organisation.'

Your answer:

____

____

____

____

____

____

____

____

____

Questions related to flight attendant duties

- **What do you think is the most important duty of a flight attendant?**

You can mention job responsibilities of a flight attendant which I have already covered in a previous chapter.

Strategic answer:

'It's a job that entails a lot of responsibilities. Flight attendants have to perform under pressure within a stipulated time frame in a professional and considerate manner. They also need to communicate in different styles that serve the needs of others. They need to carry out safety procedures and in-flight customer service as part of a team. Maintaining high grooming standards and a cheerful disposition, showing professionalism, being sensitive to the needs of special passengers and taking pride in the job are some of the major prerequisites to becoming a cabin crew member. As a cabin crew you have to meet the excellent standards of the airline in terms of customers service.'

- **What are the advantages and disadvantages of being a flight attendant?**

Answer this question by talking more about the pros and less about the cons of this job.

Strategic answer:

'Being a flight attendant, I will get the opportunity to deliver exceptional customer service. I will get to travel to different parts of the world, meet people from diverse backgrounds, and learn about their culture. Working through different time zones would, of course, be demanding. However, it will keep me challenged and active.'

Your answer:

Based on the above strategic answer, write your own:

____

____

____

____

____

____

____

- **What makes a good cabin crew?**

  Given below are the qualities that make for a good cabin crew:

  1. Cheerful disposition
  2. Good communication skills
  3. Persuasion skills
  4. Knack to serve customers in the best possible way
  5. Situation handling skills

  Strategic answer:

'A cabin crew should always sport a smile and possess great communication skills. I have excellent persuasion skills. Being able to provide good service is one of the major requirements of becoming a flight attendant, and I'm confident about my ability to provide exceptional customer experience.' (Say this with confidence and a bright smile.)

Your answer:

____

____

____

____

____

____

____

____

____

____

- **What excites/motivates you about a flight attendant's job?**

The interviewers want to ensure you haven't just come here for the salary and travel benefits and that you are a self-motivated person with a passion for customer service. Additionally, they would want to assess whether you can show empathy and go the distance to satisfy the customer's emotional needs. Keeping this in mind, answer accordingly.

Strategic answer:

'I wake up in the morning with renewed energy and zeal. I believe in having a purpose in life that challenges and motivates me. My biggest goal is to offer unmatched hospitality to a customer, and ensure they are happy and satisfied with my service. In my previous job as a relationship manager, my job was to build and maintain a great rapport with the clients; new as well as the existing ones. I was challenged and motivated to make everyday special for myself and my clients.' Then you can share an experience, if you have one, which can back up your claim.

Your answer:

____

____

____

____

____

____

____

____

____

____

____

- **How do you imagine a typical day of a cabin crew member?**

Flight attendants have no fixed time for their flights. They have to be flexible enough to fly in different zones at different times.

Strategic answer:

'This may vary depending on the airline you work for. But typically, as a cabin crew member, you have to get ready at least 2-3 hours ahead of the flight's departure. You have to board the cab, gather at a common place; a hotel or at the airport. Join other colleagues for a briefing. Then board the flight, welcome the passengers on board. After the flight has taken off, service starts and you need to serve the passengers. However, as far as timings and locations of flying are concerned, it may not be fixed. So, one has to be ready and open to fly in different cities, countries and time zones.'

Your answer:

____

____

____

____

____

____

____

____

____

____

____

____

- **What do you consider the most difficult aspect of this job?**

Every job is challenging. It has its own pros and cons. In the same fashion, flying at odd hours and in different time zones can be strenuous for some people. But the interviewers are looking for candidates who can cope up with such a situation and work happily.

Strategic answer:

'I wouldn't say it is difficult to work under different environments and time zones; rather I would say it is challenging. But then, I am open to challenges that would help me become stronger and evolve as a leader.'

Your answer:

____

____

____

____

____

____

____

____

____

____

- **What is the one thing you want to avoid in your next job?**

The interviewers want to know what you are looking for in this job. Do not say anything negative.

Strategic answer for candidates with experience:

'In my previous job, my skills were less challenged and hardly explored. I was part of the help-desk team. My job was to assist clients with check-in and check-out. So, it was a sitting job. I would like to move across cities/countries, and explore various cultures, and sometimes become a lifesaver in case of a medical emergency.'

Strategic answer for freshers:

'Sitting in a chair and making calls to clients—this is something I would not like to be a part of. I would like to work in a job where I get the opportunity to interact with people from diverse backgrounds and to provide them with exceptional customer service using my interpersonal skills. I would like to work in a team and deliver my part of service in an excellent way. Also, I am persuasive and good at convincing people. I can therefore easily sell in-flight products using my selling skills and help increase the revenue of my company and earn incentives.'

Your answer:

____

____

____

____

____

____

____

____

____

____

____

____

- **What are the challenges you are looking for in this position?**

The interviewers ask this question to check how you have handled challenges in the past, and how prepared you are for the role of a cabin crew member. This job is very challenging and one needs to be quick and adaptive at all times.

Tell your interviewers about how you have handled challenges in the past. Share an experience from your previous job which is relevant to the description of this job. If you are a fresher, select any example from your life.

Strategic answer for candidates with previous job experience:

'In my previous job, my colleague Neeta and I were given the responsibility to ensure all the orders were processed properly and delivered on time. One fine day, I noticed that Neeta was not paying attention to work and was making many errors. Due to this, I had to carry out her part of responsibilities as well.

'When I talked to her in the evening about this unusual behaviour, she told me her mother was in the hospital. After I heard this, I told her she can take permission to come late for a few days while she takes care of her mother. Then I assured her I would be able to handle the extra work in her absence and that she need not worry about work. I understand the fact that when you work as part of a team, being a good team player, and supporting and motivating other members is of absolute importance.'

Strategic answer for freshers:

'I have completed a course in how to be an effective communicator, and I am confident this would add value to my job. Apart from that, empathy and customer service skills are extremely important. I have keen interest in community work and have volunteered several times for social work. The experience has taught me to be a good human being and serve people well.'

Your answer:

____

____

____

____

____

____

____

____

____

Personality related questions

Strengths and Weakness

- **What are your strengths?**

Here you can talk about distinctive qualities you possess such as how well you can perform a task under pressure, how patient you are, and how you motivate your team members. You can mention that you are an effective listener, a problem solver, a team player, sport a positive attitude, have effective communication skills, are always eager to learn, know how to take feedback positively, are a good observer, etc. Give some examples to support your skills. Let them know why you think you have unique skills.

Tips you can use:

- Do not be overconfident. Remain humble while effectively communicating your qualities.
- Mention 3-4 traits and skills which were listed in the job description.
- Maintain your composure. Do not exaggerate.
- Share a story/experience from your previous job.

Strategic answer for those with previous job experience:

'Providing exceptional customer service is my passion. I can perform under pressure and finish my tasks within a tight schedule. In my previous job at a restaurant, I used to be part of a food-processing team where I had to process many orders within a stipulated time frame. I always adhered to the standards set by the company.'

Strategic answer for freshers:

'I am a football player. Being part of a football team taught me how to be quick at decision-making and be a team player. This is something that one learns when you have to plan and pass on the ball to your team-mate, a calculation that ends up deciding the fate of the team. I also learnt to be accountable for my actions and deliver my part of the job sincerely and exceptionally. Not just this, conflict resolution using interpersonal skills come naturally to me.'

Your answer:

Based on the above strategy, write your answer here:

- **What is your greatest weakness?**

This is a behavioural question and can put you in an uncomfortable position. To attempt answering such a question, never say you don't have any weaknesses. You have to basically convey that you are aware of your weaknesses and take corrective actions to overcome them. The motive behind asking such a question is to avoid the risks of a bad hire.

Tips you can use:

- Don't be dishonest. Pick up a weakness which you can genuinely improve, such as technical skills, public-speaking skills, time management, etc.
- Tell them what measures you took to correct your weakness.
- End on a positive note.

Strategic answer for those with previous job experience:

'Multi-tasking is a problem for me. I used to focus all my concentration on one part of the job. At times, I would be required to oversee multiple tasks at once, which would leave me flustered. To avoid making mistakes, I took measures to ensure I was delivering the work on time. I set aside time slots to complete the tasks. I also wrote down to-do lists and set reminders to increase my efficiency. I can proudly say I manage my time better now and even multitask.'

Strategic answer for freshers:

'I am not an expert on computers. Using Microsoft Office was a bit of a challenge initially, but then I joined a course and developed my computer skills. I am improving every day to get closer to perfection.'

- **What is the one negative thing that your friend or your last boss said about you?**

Here the interviewers want to check your weaknesses. Think about an example such as being a workaholic, fitness freak, or obsessive organiser. At first, mention it as your weakness and then turn it to your advantage.

Strategic answer:

'I know being a workaholic means you kind of disconnect from the world. That's what my boss used to say since I avoided office parties and any chance to socialise due to work. Between work and partying, I always chose work. But later, I realised, something was missing. Hence, I started to put in an effort to strike a balance between my work and social life.'

Your answer:

____

____

____

____

____

____

____

____

____

____

- **How do you rate your communication skills on a scale of 1-10?**

Communication skills are very important to customer service. Since we all know that nobody is perfect and there is always room for improvement, give yourself between 8 to 9.5 out of 10. You don't want to give yourself 6 or 7 because then you would not look like a perfect candidate. It is also significant to work upon communication skills constantly.

Strategic answer:

'I rate myself as a good communicator and I can give myself a 9/10. But then, I also understand when it comes to communication skills there is always room for improvement. And I am open to any feedback. Moreover, I always try to be as precise and clear as possible in my communication.'

Your answer:

____

____

____

____

____

____

____

____

____

____

Attitudinal Questions

- **Are you a team player?**

Team work plays a key role amongst cabin crew members. It's integral to the successful execution of their jobs. So when you are asked this question, do not just say, 'Yes, I am a team player.' Share an experience to prove how you are one.

Strategic answer for those with previous job experience:

'In my previous organisation I was part of a four-member team. My job was to process the application form once the verifier had verified the authenticity of the information provided in it. One day, my colleague who used to verify the form fell sick and the work got stuck. Being highly aware of the deadlines, and realising that our clients would be disappointed if they do not get the required documents on time, I got into action mode. I was happy to take the initiative and decided to myself verify the details and process the form. I thus ensured that my team didn't suffer and was happy to provide the completed work to a satisfied client.'

Strategic answer for freshers:

'Yes, I am very much a team player. I have had several opportunities to work within a team during my school and college days. It helped me to work within group dynamics and bring out my strengths as well as that of the others in the team.'

You can mention the project and how you played a key role as a team member. Further, talk about the power of a team over an individual, and about how a team can achieve much more and work together to find solutions for every problem. You can also add that during your in-house training program on team building, you were taught the nitty-gritties of team building (say this only if you have attended any team building program).

- **Are you a social person?**

Socialising doesn't just mean partying or gossiping. It also doesn't mean spending time on social networking sites. It means being among people, doing some social activities, helping each other, and having fun together but not wasting a whole lot of time doing that.

Strategic answer:

'Yes, I am a fun-loving and outgoing person. I love to be around people, and contribute to community work. However, I always remain focused on my ultimate goal.'

Your answer:

____

____

____

____

____

____

____

- **How do you deal with failure?**

Optimistic people always look at failures as stepping stones for their success.

Strategic answer:

'To me failures are like great teachers in my life. They've not only taught me some great lessons, but have thrown me into challenging situations that have nudged me to achieve something bigger in life. The fact of the matter is if one wants to become successful, one must be ready to face bigger setbacks in life.'

Your answer:

- **How do you handle pressure?**

OR

Are you able to work under pressure?

To answer that question, you can give an example of an incident that happened at your previous job or cite one from your life when you were under high pressure, and how you managed it.

Strategic answer for those with previous job experience:

At times pressure brings out the best in you. When you have deadlines to meet, you tend to focus more. You pull up your socks and put in an extra effort to deliver your best especially when time is short. Now, imagine if a person puts the same amount of effort every single day; he would achieve the pinnacle of success sooner rather than later. That's what winners do. In my previous organisation, I came across a situation where we needed to deliver our shipments within 15 days. However, a few of our machines broke down and it took 2 days to get them repaired. We had to extend our shifts for 2 hours daily to cover the deadline. We not only completed the assignments on time, but also maintained our quality standards.'

Strategic answer for freshers:

'I always see working under pressure as an opportunity to grow as a person. I know that every time I have worked under pressure, it has given me a unique experience and made me stronger. It also helps to bring out the best in me. In real life, things change for the best under intense pressure, starting from cooking food to moulding an iron.

'When I was in college, I fell sick just 2 months before the exams. It was really bothering me because I was not able to concentrate on my studies. But after a few days, when I recovered from my illness, I studied as though I had to run and win a marathon. I knew in my heart, I had the stamina and potential to complete my studies in the limited time I was left with. Finally, I passed with flying colours.'

Your answer:

Share a story of when you worked under pressure and how you dealt with it. Also, add two benefits you got or lessons you learnt from that incident.

- **How do you deal with criticism?**

A majority of people are very sensitive to criticism. They take it personally and feel disheartened. However, strong people always take criticism positively. If they come across any irrelevant or obnoxious comment, they simply ignore it. But a person who truly wants to improve will work on their weaknesses and learn from their mistakes.

Strategic answer:

'I think without strong critics, no great work would have ever been created. I am open to feedback. I look at it as an opportunity to work on my weak points so that I am well prepared the next time. Once, when I had to make a presentation in front of my colleagues, it didn't go as planned. Even though I received encouraging feedback from my colleagues as well as my boss, they also shared some useful tips with me on how to improve my presentations skills.

'I took their advice seriously and worked relentlessly on my presentation skills. My hard work paid off when I received a lot more of appreciation from my colleagues and boss the next time I made a presentation. Safe to say, I am open to constructive criticism as it gives me room to work on myself.'

Your answer:

- **Do you prefer to work independently or in a team?**

Remember cabin crew have to work in a large group. A key requirement for this job is to work in a team environment.

Do not say that it depends on the situation. That may reduce your chances of getting selected over other candidates.

Strategic answer:

'I am an enthusiastic team player and prefer working in a team. However, I can also work independently.'

Your answer:

Write about your experience when you worked as a team and as an individual.

___

___

___

___

___

___

___

___

___

___

- **What motivates you to do your best on the job?**

It could be one or many reasons that can motivate a person to do well in his job. It could be recognition, a sense of achievement, perks, etc. But the hiring managers are looking for something unique. So, give an answer that makes you stand out.

Strategic answer:

'I am passionate about making a difference to people's lives. I'm confident in my ability to make someone's day better. That's what motivates me to add value. In my previous job, I used to take orders for pizza. During the few seconds of taking the order, I used to smile genuinely and make the customers feel happy. This instantly created a rapport between the customers and they left feeling validated.'

Your answer:

Write strong reasons that keep you motivated.

___

___

___

___

___

___

___

___

___

___

___

- **Did you go through any major change in life? If yes, how did you handle it?**

Talk about an incident that completely changed your life. It can be something from your personal life or something your loved one went through. If possible, take a negative incident and later mention about the lessons you learned from it. Write the following: What was the incident? When did it happen? What change did it bring to your life? What were the important life lessons you learnt? But make sure your answer is in accordance with the airline's objectives. Show them what they want to see, tell them what they want to hear.

Your answer:

____

____

____

____

____

____

____

____

____

____

Goals and Achievements

- **Where do you see yourself 5 to 10 years from now?**

You can do a bit of research about the hierarchy that the airlines follow. With such a question, the hiring managers aim to judge whether you have seriously given a thought to your career options.

Strategic answer:

'In life, growth is essential, and I would like to develop my skills and evolve within this profession. Having said that, I would like to grow more as an individual, in terms of modesty, efficiency, and always going the extra mile to deliver unmatched customer service. I would like to become a team leader where I can utilize my skills and experience to create more leaders like me within the organisation. However, at the end of the day, I would always carry out my duties diligently and work towards maintaining the highest standards.'

Your answer:

Based on the above strategic answer, write your own answer:

Points to remember: *You should always be prepared for cross questions; the recruiters may ask tricky questions to gauge whether you've memorised the answers or if you're really passionate about the job.*

- **What is your biggest goal in life?**

Use diplomacy when answering such a question. Remember recruiters are experienced, and they can see through your flattery, and may not be impressed with your choice of answer. However, if your answer reflects a passion for something else other than cabin crew, then you may have landed yourself in a puddle. Remember to strike a balance between the two.

Strategic answer:

'Right now my biggest goal is to find myself a dream job that will give me an opportunity to travel, discover different cultures and meet interesting people from various nations and find an opportunity to serve them. It is an ideal job that would be challenging and exciting at the same time.'

Your answer:

Why don't you just try writing about that. It will be fun and will give you good insights about your personality.

____

____

____

____

____

____

____

____

____

____

- **What is your greatest accomplishment?**

By asking this question, the interviewers want to know what value you bring to the organisation. This is an opportunity for you to share your accomplishments that you think can be most valuable for them. For this question, make a list of 2-3 of your accomplishments and their impact. How were you able to help the company? Use the S-T-A-R (the Situation you faced, the Task required, the Action you took, and the successful Result of your action) technique to describe your achievement. The STAR questions are explained in detail in the chapter titled 'The STAR Technique'.

Strategic answer for those who have previous job experience:

'In my previous job, when I was handling customer service, I came across an irate customer. He was 65 and though his issue had been resolved, he wanted some compensation which was not possible. I calmly listened to his grievances without interrupting him, and showed empathy. In the end, I gave him an explanation and tried to make him understand why providing compensation was not possible. After that, the customer was satisfied, and did not ask for any compensation.'

Strategic answer for freshers:

'I couldn't speak English fluently till a few months ago. However, I did not let that become a deterrent in my life. Instead, I put in a lot of effort and worked relentlessly on my language skills. I can now confidently say I am fluent in English.'

This can also be a great accomplishment. Don't think that an achievement needs to be grandiose to be mentioned.

Your answer:

List a few of your greatest achievements here:

Behavioural Interview Questions

To answer such questions effectively, you can use Situation, Action, Result (SAR). The SAR (or STAR) method is a very useful preparation technique to describe your achievements in a coherent, structured manner.

- **Why did you leave your last job?**

You need to be careful while answering this question. Just remember one thing; never say anything negative about your previous or current employer. You don't want to give an impression that a few years later, you could be saying the same thing about them after you are hired.

Further, even though one of the major reasons for you to apply for a cabin crew position is financial stability, do not mention this to the recruiter. The recruiters are already aware of the salary incentive and are interested to see what you can bring to the table.

Strategic answer:

'I was doing well professionally, however, I realised that I am more suited to work in a challenging environment within a team set-up which will help me evolve professionally and as an individual.'

Then talk about a few responsibilities that a flight attendant has and your job did not have. 'As a flight attendant, I would be responsible for the safety of passengers, initiate life-saving procedures in case of a life-threatening situation. That's what makes this job more appealing. Not only that, this job gives you global exposure. You get to meet people with different cultures and backgrounds.'

Your answer:

- **Have you ever had a conflict with someone? How was it resolved?**

Strategic answer for those with previous job experience:

'It was more of a disagreement over a few things with my colleagues. I believe conflicts occur when there is a difference in opinion. When conflicts occur, I try to listen to the perspective of others, analyse them and try to resolve the issue amicably. If the need arises, I immediately take the issue to the manager and get it resolved.

'In my previous organisation, my colleague Rahul was making slow progress in his work. Due to this, we were behind our deadlines and work schedule. I took Rahul in confidence and tried to understand the real cause behind it. He told me that he was unhappy due to the appraisal which had taken place a few days ago. He was expecting a bigger increment in his salary. I tried to explain to him how his behaviour was unacceptable, and could result in him losing his job. And that if his hard work would show through his performance, he is more likely to get a better hike next time. He got my point and we were back on schedule.'

Let's put this incident in a SAR or STAR (Situation or Task, Action, Result) format to understand clearly.

Situation: Rahul was making slow progress. Due to this, the team was behind schedule.

Action: You won the confidence of Rahul first, understood the real cause for the slow pace of work and explained to him the benefits of hard work and consequences of not working well.

Result: Rahul got back to working properly and the task was completed on time.

- **Tell me about a time when you disagreed with your boss?**

Be extremely careful here. You don't want to leave a negative impression on the interviewers by bashing your previous boss.

Strategic answer:

'It's not really easy to confront your manager. However, at times it is a good strategy, keeping in mind the benefits it might give to the team and organisation. In my previous organisation, we were losing customers because there was no installment facility. I brought this matter to the attention of my boss but initially, he wasn't in agreement with me. Later, he understood the importance of this plan and how it would help maximise sales and help us give better services to our prospective clients. So, he implemented it.'

Let's put it in a SAR or STAR format to understand it clearly.

Situation: Sharp decline in number of customers due to lack of EMI facility.

Action: You brought the matter to the attention of the concerned person and made your point.

Result: The EMI facility was made available to the clients.

Your answer:

___

___

___

___

___

___

___

___

___

___

- **Have you ever worked with someone you didn't like? If so, how did you handle it?**

It is human tendency to have a certain perception about some people. Sometimes you are required to work with a person you don't like. However, when you are working as a flight attendant, you need to be professional and keep the team environment healthy and happy. You need to learn how to differentiate between personal and professional issues. So, your approach to this answer should be well-thought-out as this is again a tricky question.

Strategic answer:

'Whenever any issue came up, I immediately took action and resolved it amicably. If required, I took the matter to my manager and sorted it out instantly. It is quite natural to have difference of opinions when you are working together, but that has nothing to do with liking or disliking a person. So, my strong belief is that any matter can be resolved when we can sit and talk to understand each other's point of view.'

Your answer:

- **What was the one thing you disliked the most at your previous job?**

This is a question asked to determine how you evaluate unpleasant moments when working in a professional setup. Your interviewer is looking for a negative answer. Do not say anything negative about your previous job. They wouldn't want to ruin their company image by hiring employees who don't believe in the vision of the company they work in and badmouth the organisation.

Strategic answer:

'Even though my previous job proved to be a great learning curve, I realised soon enough it didn't have the scope for a more global reach and provided even lesser opportunities for growth. It was restricting my career trajectory, and was often unchallenging. When I got to know about the opportunities that this job offered, I got excited and found myself as the perfect candidate.'

Your answer:

____

____

____

____

____

____

____

____

____

- **When have you been flexible in a previous work situation?**

Being flexible is one of the most important qualities required of a cabin crew. They have to operate flights under different environments. If you have worked in different timings in your previous job, you can mention that or you can give an example from your life that shows how flexible you are.

Strategic answer:

'In my previous job, I had rotational shifts that changed every fortnight. At times I had to do morning shifts and then after 15 days I had to do night shifts. It was an organisation that dealt in travel and tourism and had offices globally. I quickly adapted to the changing work schedules and maintained the standards of the organisation.'

Your answer:

____

____

____

____

____

____

____

____

____

____

____

- **Have you had to change your communication style to get your point across?**

Think of a situation wherein you had to interact with a mixed group in a family or an organisational setup. You cannot use the same style of communication with children, youth and senior members. This question is asked to check if you are able to deal with people from different age groups because cabin crew members have to serve diverse people.

Here's an example you can use to design your own answer based on your work or life's experience.

Strategic answer for those with previous job experience:

'In my previous organisation, I happened to encounter an elderly customer who was unfamiliar with the process of withdrawing money. I patiently walked him through the technicalities, and even offered to write down the information on a piece of paper, in case he forgets. He understood and happily obliged.'

Let's put the strategic answer in a SAR format.

Situation: Customer was not able to understand the technical process of withdrawing money.

Action: I changed my communication style and explained the process in layman terms.

Result: The customer got the point and left happily.

Situational Interview Question

- **What would you do if a passenger was impolite?**

Sometimes you need to deal with impolite and impatient passengers. In that case, patience is the key to success. You have to be firm, polite and patient to understand the passenger's position. You have to listen to the passenger's problems, and provide solutions as quickly as possible.

Strategic answer:

'First I would hear him/her attentively and patiently. I will show empathy, and acknowledge the problem. Once he or she has completed speaking, I would try to give an immediate solution within my capacity. If required, I would immediately contact the supervisor and get the issue resolved. My goal would be to ensure that my customer is satisfied with my customer service.'

Your answer:

____

____

____

____

____

____

____

- **If a passenger is scared of flying, what would you say?**

First-timers or people who have flying phobia are usually very anxious and nervous, and to handle such passengers requires patience and skill.

Strategic answer:

'Judging by their state of mind, I will try to help them relax by engaging them in a pleasant conversation. I will enquire if they're first-time flyers, and explain in detail the safety protocols of the aircraft. I will assure them that there is nothing to worry about and also demonstrate the experiences of first-time flyers to help them loosen up a bit more.'

Your answer:

____

____

____

____

____

____

____

- **If a passenger came into the airplane very upset and crying, how would you handle it?**

Human beings are very emotional. At times when we are hurt, we want to express our emotions by crying or we simply keep thinking about the bad incidents that happened which make us upset.

Strategic answer:

'I will ask the passenger about the matter and pacify him. Then I will also tell him that he may reach me at any point in time by pressing the flight attendant call button. I will also keep on visiting him during intervals to check on his mental status.'

Your answer:

____

____

____

____

____

____

____

- **How would you motivate others?**

Give an example from a real-life incident where you were able to motivate others to complete a particular project or task. Flight attendants face many challenging situations during the course of their jobs, and to keep a smiling face and behave patiently and skillfully requires a high level of inner motivation. The interviewer wants to check whether you are capable of motivating others in case it is needed. Use the STAR method to answer such behavioural questions.

Be confident about your answer and give a well-structured reply complemented by appropriate body language. It won't be a bad idea to study the core values of the airline you have applied to and model your answer around that. For example, if the airline gives highest priority to customer service, which most of the airlines do, pick an answer or experience from your life that complements this.

Strategic answer for those with previous work experience:

'In my previous organisation, we were a team of four people who were handling guest relations. At the end of our shifts, we needed to handover our work to the person who handled the next shift. One of our colleagues seemed to make a lot of errors while handing over. When I asked her the reason for such behaviour, she told me all her hardwork was going unnoticed. I assured her that good work will be recognised eventually and she would be praised for her work. But if she continues doing poor work, she may lose her credibility and the job as well. She understood my point and put in more effort. And the best part is that she was promoted after 5 months.' (Try to smile here when you are making a good, solid finish.)

Strategic answer for freshers:

'During my college years, 3 of my friends and I decided to study together as a group before the exam. One of my friends seemed to lag behind in Accountancy. When I asked him the reason behind his slow pace, he opened up about not understanding some of the concepts. When I got to know this, I ensured we were all on the same page, and after consulting with other group members, slowed down the pace at which we were covering our lessons, so that he could catch up with us.'

Your answer:

____

____

____

____

____

____

____

- **How would you deal with being away from your friends and family for a long period of time when working as a cabin crew?**

If you are selected for an international airline, its base may not be in the country you belong to. You may have to live in Doha or any other country depending on where the airline is based. You will have to fly to different international destinations from there. So, sometimes it becomes really difficult to cope with feelings of loneliness, adjusting to a new environment, and staying without family or friends for extended time periods. You will not only have to deal with emotionally difficult phases but also meet the demands of the job with perfection.

Strategic answer:

'As a flight attendant, I'm cognizant of the demands and expectations placed on me. Even though I will be staying away from my family and friends, I will always prioritise my career, and ensure I'm not shirking my responsibilities.'

Your answer:

____

____

____

____

____

____

____

____

- **How will you ensure a happy environment on board?**

Despite the long-hours and strenuous working conditions, cabin crew has to maintain a cheerful countenance at all times. Greeting customers and resolving their issues with genuine eagerness always goes a long way. Recruiters can easily detect when a candidate is unenthusiastic.

Strategic answer:

'A smile spreads positivity around us. When we enjoy our work and serve people with a smile, it makes the whole environment lively. I love people and I love myself. So, I think these two qualities will make the environment conducive on board.'

Your answer:

You may also like to share any example from your previous organisation or any life event.

___

___

___

___

___

___

___

___

___

- **Give me an example of a time when you had to conform to a policy you did not agree with.**

This type of question is called 'disagree and commit'. At times, you do not agree with certain orders depending on your values and desires. However, this job has certain standards and norms which one may need to follow even when you might not be in agreement with it personally. The interviewers want to see how you manage such situations and perform your duties.

Strategic answer:

'In my previous organisation, due to the shortage of employees and high work pressure, my supervisors used to ask me to work overtime every day. The problem was that there was no office cab available after office hours. So, I had to go home on my own, travelling by bus for 45 minutes.

'Even though it was a strenuous time, coupled with the gruelling journey back home, I only opted for a day off. I took on extra responsibilities to help without demanding any incentive. This continued for a while till the company had enough personnel to work during the allotted time.'

- **What do you expect from a supervisor?**

This is again a tricky question. As a candidate you have no idea about the work style of your future boss. Also, you do not want to get emotional and take out the frustration of what you might have endured in your previous job onto the current recruiters. Answer this question smartly and show that you can work efficiently without having any problem with your immediate supervisor.

Strategic answer:

'Favouritism is the biggest killer of motivation. In my previous organisation, everyone was given a fair opportunity to learn and grow within the organisation. My boss always had a personal rapport with the employees. Such an environment works well for the mutual growth of employees and the organisation.'

Your answer:

____

____

____

____

____

____

____

- **How would you react if we asked you to change your appearance completely to fit in at our company?**

You must understand that you are applying for a flight attendant's job, which is known for the good looks and glamour associated with it. Every effort made to groom a candidate for his/her appearance or skills are always in the best interests of the candidates and the organisations.

Strategic answer:

'Well, I know for a fact that there is always room for betterment. If the organisation wants any change in my appearance, that will be for the highest good for both myself and the organisation. Therefore, I will be more than willing to adapt to the change whether it's in my appearance or skills.'

Your answer:

____

____

____

____

____

____

____

____

- **If you smell alcohol on the captain's breath, what will you do about it?**

Although this is a hypothetical situation, it is a critical issue. It may cost the life of hundreds of people on board and is a matter of great concern. But then, there has to be some procedure that you need to follow as a flight attendant. The best thing you can do is inform the supervisor or flight emcee.

Strategic answer:

'Such a situation can be life threatening. In this case, I would inform my supervisor. I cannot say with surety if the captain has consumed alcohol or not but if I feel suspicious it is my responsibility to ensure safety protocols are being followed on board. I would seek the flight emcee's intervention in the matter.'

Your answer:

____

____

____

____

____

____

____

____

____

- **Give me an example of a time when you did not agree with your supervisor. What was it and what did you do?**

The interviewer is looking for a candidate who can fit in their organisation. When you are working together, disagreements are part of the job. 9 out of 10 times, you can agree. But there may come a time when you do not see eye to eye.

Strategic answer:

'In my previous organisation, I disagreed with my supervisor over helping an irate customer by going beyond the policy of the company. I told him why I waived off 10% of the charges and how happy it made the customer. Earlier the customer was going to our rival company but now with mutual trust and understanding, he prefers to come to us. In the long run, such an exchange will be highly profitable for the firm. I also apologised for not seeking his advise over the matter and assured him of complete faith in exercising authority.'

- **If I were your supervisor and asked you to do something you disagreed with, what would you do?**

In this case, it is more about handling a conflict smartly. At times, you are asked to do some work which may not be within your area of responsibility. You have to leave behind your inhibitions if your job demands that.

Strategic answer:

'I would always like to be in sync with my supervisor. I know that when I am on the job, I have to be ready to perform my duties as best as I can. However, if for any reason, I disagree with you as a supervisor, I would explain my side of the story to you and look for a middle ground. In my previous organisation, I had a small disagreement about firing an employee who gave an unsatisfactory performance for three months in a row. I explained to my supervisor why sending him for retraining would be for the benefit of the employee and the company. He understood my point and agreed to retrain him and give him another chance.'

Your answer:

___

___

___

___

___

___

___

___

___

Questions about the Organisation

- **Do you know what types of aircraft we fly?**

Do a little bit of research on the airline company you have applied to and find out about the types of aircraft they fly. Also, explore the benefits, the comfort level of those particular aircraft and learn a little about their functioning.

Your notes:

Select any airline of your choice and research on it. Write down the types of aircraft they fly and the destinations they cover.

____

____

____

____

____

____

____

____

____

____

- **Why did you choose this particular airline?**

OR

Why do you want to work with us?

The hiring managers want to know how much you know about the company culture, its values, vision, etc.

You must research to get some valuable information about the airline. Visit their official website and get to know about their culture, values, and their presence. You can also access Google and YouTube to get more information and the latest news on the company. Try to find out information which may not be available on their website such as news on some achievements, mergers, acquisitions, awards, etc.

To give an answer you need to mention the kind of culture they have, such as a safe environment for employees, the amount of learning and professional growth they provide, etc. You can also match some of your values with theirs. For example, one of their values could be 'outstanding customer service'. You can say how much you are willing to serve the passengers in the best possible way.

When you participate in airline open days, you will get to see a display wherein you will see a series of videos about the airline, their establishment date, their presence, and history. It would be a good idea to take some notes from there.

Your answer:

Select any airline of your choice and do some research. Write their mission statement, establishment date, core values, their global presence, etc. Collect as much information as you can and write it below:

- **What do you know about our company?**

To answer this question, visit the website of the company, search on Google using keywords such as 'news about <followed by the company's name>', 'press releases <followed by the company name>'. Next, you can visit their LinkedIn and Facebook pages. Once you have done all of these, you can compile the information. Given below is a list I created that will help you in your research:

➢ How long has the company been in existence
➢ What type of aircraft the company owns
➢ What kind of products and services the company offers
➢ What their company culture is like
➢ What the company's mission and vision statements are

Strategic answer:

'Your airline has a good reputation in the industry. It operates from Singapore and covers multiple destinations across the globe. The company was established in the year________ and since then it has flourished. It owns various types of aircraft mainly Airbus and Boeing. The company believes in excellent customer service and providing a healthy environment to its employees. The company's mission is to________________________.'

Your answer:

- **How do you feel wearing a uniform at work?**

Wearing a cabin crew uniform is your dream. Tell the interviewers how you love those uniforms especially the one that is worn at the airline you have applied to. Know the colour and design of their uniform. You can see it on their official website or the advertisement in the newspaper. See how they promote a cabin crew wearing the uniform with a bright smile and a sense of pride.

Sample answer:

'I love to be recognised and mark my own identity with the name of my organisation I am working for. A uniform is an identity which gives me a sense of pride and keeps reminding me about the responsibilities I hold. For example, what is the need for the Indian Army or Indian Air Force to wear uniforms? It gives them pride, motivation and helps them stay focused. Moreover, I love the colour and design of the uniform which is of_______________. (Explain in detail the uniform of that airline which will show your keen interest in their company.)

Your answer:

____

____

____

____

____

____

____

____

____

____

____

- **How many nights did you spend in a hotel or away from home last year?**

Here you can talk about any travel experience where you stayed away from home for a considerable period of time. You can say how much you enjoy going on a vacation or being away from home occasionally. If you are already away from your home for your studies or work, you can discuss that.

Interviewers ask this question to find out whether you are capable of coping with emotional pain which may occur for some people when they are away from their loved ones for long periods of time. Some airlines have their base in their home country. For example, Singapore Airlines operates from Singapore. So, even though you are an Indian national, you will need to stay outside your country.

Strategic answer:

'In my last job, I was sent to Delhi to complete a task. It was a 7-day trip and I had to stay in a hotel which was provided by my company. I felt independent and even more responsible. Even though I missed my family, technology helped me stay connected with them through video calls and messages.'

Your answer:

____

____

____

____

____

____

____

____

____

- **Are you willing to relocate?**

This job might require you to relocate to metro cities within the country or outside the country from where the airline operates. Hence, you will be expected to be ready for the relocation. This might be one of the major requirements of the airline. Thus, give a significant reason why you are more than willing to relocate. If you are staying away from your parents, it would not be difficult for you to convince the hiring managers. However, if you have never stayed away from your family, find a valid reason to make them believe that this is something you can easily and willingly do.

Strategic answer:

'I stayed in Delhi for a couple of weeks during my course in communication skills. I must say that it was a good experience. I did not like it initially because staying away from your family and friends is not that easy. But then, I believe this kind of experience is mandatory to help you grow as a person and become more independent. I learnt a lot of things about my own personality, about the world, and felt more responsible towards my job and duties. If given a chance, I would be more than willing to relocate.'

Remember: This is a sample answer based on which you can prepare your own.

Your notes:

Write strong reasons for your relocation.

____

____

____

____

____

____

____

Your answer:

____

____

____

____

____

____

____

____

____

____

____

- **Why do you believe that you can be a better flight attendant?**

  OR

  Why should we hire you?

Here you can talk about your qualifications and unique qualities. Talk about your strengths at large. If you have some prior customer service experience, or if you know any foreign language, this is a good time to mention that.

Strategic answer:

'I am excellent at building a rapport quickly and have great communication skills. My ability to upsell products in my previous organisation has resulted in fabulous sales figures. I have always made my organisation proud and profitable. Moreover, I am quite capable of coping with challenging situations. I can work in a team as well as independently. I am a go-getter. So, I think I am perfect for this job.'

Your answer:

- **What does customer service mean to you?**

The chief aim of cabin crew members is to deliver exceptional customer service. With this question, the interviewers would want to gauge your attitude towards customer service.

Strategic answer:

'Customer service is more than just fulfilling a set of responsibilities. It means ensuring the customers smile. It means making the trip memorable for the passengers by providing them great customer service, being courteous, showing empathy so that they come back to fly with us in the future and recommend our services to others. It also means ensuring safety, being sensitive to special passengers, and sensing the needs of customers even before they ask for it.'

Your answer:

- **What are your salary expectations?**

It is advisable to have some prior information about the remuneration scale offered in this profile by the airlines.

A safe answer to give would be: 'I will go as per the norms of the company.' However, if you can mention any figure that will make you sound like a well-informed candidate in the eye of the interviewers, that would be great too. At times, airlines do mention the salary range in their advertisement for cabin crew positions. In case you don't have much of an idea, you can go to online job portals and search the salary range for the position you have applied for.

Strategic answer for those with previous job experience:

'My salary expectations are in line with my qualifications and work experience. However, as per the industry standards, I am looking for a salary between INR 5 lacs to 5.50 lacs annually, but I am open to negotiate the salary depending on benefits, and other opportunities.'

Strategic answer for freshers:

'My salary expectations are in line with my qualifications. I am sure we can come to an agreement where the company can offer me the best as per the industry standard.'

Your answer:

____

____

____

____

____

____

____

____

____

____

Author's Note

The questions listed above are for your reference. Use them for guidance purpose only, and do not learn them by heart. Use your common sense and mould your answer according to your personality, background and experiences.

Every question asked during an interview is aimed at determining your suitability for the job. No answer is right or wrong but it has to be relevant. Just be yourself and give answers that reflect wisdom and presence of mind. You must also be aware of the roles and responsibilities of a flight attendant, and the qualities required to perform well under that role.

While answering the interview questions, please keep the following in mind:

- Speak confidently and clearly while answering each

question. Do not make sounds like um, ah, well, etc. Instead, learn filler words when you're thinking of an answer.

- Do take a pause in between while speaking.
- Do not give scripted answers. Do not learn the answers by heart. Sound natural.
- Be specific and stick to the point.
- Show that you understand the roles and responsibilities of this job very well.
- Never give your answer in just one word like 'Yes' or 'No' unless it is required.
- Don't fake it. If you are not sure about an answer or do not understand a question, just be honest and say so.

Debunking Myths: Busting Preconceived Notions about Flying

Not everything we hear holds truth. But then how many people really bother to verify the authenticity of all the information that comes their way? When we don't question and validate misinformation or rumours that we hear through various mediums, there are high chances of us unconsciously accepting them as true. Later, this becomes a part of our beliefs and these beliefs work like mental blocks, stopping us from moving ahead in life. Such beliefs are called limiting beliefs.

There are a lot of things that you might have heard or read about the job of a flight attendant. While most of what you've heard about flying may hold true, a lot of it is just hearsay. Do not let unverified information become the only truth and stop you from chasing your dreams. I am going to bust some of those myths for you:

Myth No. 1: To become a flight attendant, you need to have extraordinary looks

A flight attendant must be presentable as it is a customer-focused industry. Your main job is to ensure the safety of the passengers inside the aircraft and offer them great customer service. In order to perform those tasks effectively, you need to possess certain skills. The point I want to make here is that attitude and passion towards your dream job should reflect in your actions. So, candidates with average looks have the same chance of getting selected over other candidates with extraordinary looks. The only thing you need to keep in mind is that you must not have any visible marks, scars and tattoos. The rest depends on your skills.

Myth No. 2: Prior experience is mandatory to apply for the job

Every airline has its own standards that they set as a part of their selection process. There are many airlines that recruit freshers as well. A candidate who has successfully completed higher secondary or 12th standard and above meets the criteria set by the airline and is eligible to apply. Having prior experience in handling customers would of course be an added advantage. For instance, the work experience of serving customers in the hospitality industry or working as a ground staff at the airport will certainly help but it is not mandatory.

Myth No. 3: You should be slim and tall

There is no perfect definition of being slim or tall. If your height and weight are as per the airline's standards, it suffices the purpose in order to apply for the job. You should look presentable and your body language should be positive. One can always work on the appearance and improve. You need to have an average height and weight in proportion.

Moreover, you should be healthy and fit to carry out certain responsibilities of the job.

Myth No. 4: You must join an air hostess academy to get selected as a flight attendant

It is up to you whether you are willing to join an air hostess academy or not. If you join an air hostess academy, you may learn several important aspects of the responsibilities of cabin crew during your course. However, it does not guarantee your selection as a flight attendant in any airline. Alternatively, you may choose to attend some courses on grooming, personality development, spoken English, etc., which will certainly increase your chances of getting selected.

Myth No. 5: Candidates coming from metro cities are the first choice of any airline

I am a small-town girl myself and it is absolutely fine if you too come from a small city. Your home town has nothing to do with your selection. You should be the right fit. That's about it. Nothing else matters. Nowadays a few airlines may ask you for a local address which should be in a metro city. In that case, I suggest providing the address of any relative or friend for correspondence.

You may also choose to move to any one of the metro cities near you. It will be an added advantage. This will help you get accustomed to city life. Additionally, it will reduce your travel time, and you can appear for several airline interviews within the city. The fact of the matter is that most airlines conduct their interviews in metro cities. However, changing your whereabouts is completely your choice.

Myth No. 6: As a flight attendant you get to develop habits such as smoking and drinking alcohol

How we grow as a person is always in our hands. After you have got the job, it is always a matter of choice. No one ever forces you to smoke or drink. No industry is good or bad. It is you who can choose to do what is best for you.

Myth No. 7: Flight attendants are basically waitresses/waiters in the sky

There is much more to this job than what meets the eye. Serving snacks and drinks to the passengers is one of the many responsibilities of the cabin crew. The most important role of flight attendants is the safety of passengers. If anything goes wrong at 30,000 feet and above, it is just you and your co-workers who have to handle the situation. During any emergency he or she can quickly go from being a smiling, caring cabin crew member to a fire fighter, a nurse and a life saver. Handling a drunk or an unruly passenger who can be a threat to the safety and the wellbeing of others is another important part of their duty and is often performed professionally. Cabin crew are trained to handle life-threatening circumstances.

A cabin crew can revive a person with no pulse and heartbeat.

Isn't it a respectful job?

I have handled many such situations in my career and take immense pride in helping others.

Myth No. 8: Cabin crew members are required to compromise with their values

You are never forced to do anything against your will or values. This job requires you to live all alone in another city or country. So, you must be strong, confident, and capable enough to handle any undesirable situation. You should know your rights and limits. There is a system by which you can forward your concern, if you come across any unwanted situation or face harassment at work. And it is applicable to both male as well as female cabin crew.

Myth No. 9: The career of a flight attendant gets over within 8-10 years

I have been flying for over a decade now. My job is secured until I retire. Hence, you can imagine yourself working as a flight attendant long term. Although the retirement age varies for different airlines, domestic airlines in India have marked 42-48 years as the age of retirement whereas international airlines allow the crew members to work until the age of 58-62 years and even more. What an airline expects from you is to keep yourself fit and healthy to carry out the responsibilities of the job efficiently. This is considered to be one of the most likable career options for young candidates. So, don't believe in the rumours that people might peddle your way and start working towards this long-term and exciting career.

Myth No. 10: Marriage and pregnancy are hurdles to this job

Most of the airlines prefer to take young freshers who can give a few uninterrupted years to the company. A few Middle-East carriers also ask you to sign a contract stating that you will stay unmarried for the first few years. Once that period gets over, you are allowed to get married and can avail the pregnancy benefits too. The benefits are given as per the company policy. For example paid and unpaid leave, health insurance and work as ground crew.

After a certain period set by the company, you can join back.

Myth No. 11: One needs a recommendation to get the job

Airlines are very particular about the selection of their employees as they want someone who strictly adheres to the standards set by the company. If a candidate does not fit the required criteria asked by the airline, he/she is not entertained.

All the candidates have to go through the same selection process and prove their abilities. An employee has to be an asset to the company, especially one that involves customer service. Hence the hiring is done keeping that in mind.

I have not come across anyone who came on board through references or favours. So my advice is to believe in yourself, work on your shortcomings, improve your personality and fly high.

Myth No. 12: Knowledge of a foreign language is a must

Firstly, you do not need to know a foreign language to apply for domestic carriers. However, if you do know any regional language, that would be considered an added advantage. Similarly, international airlines hire Indian flight attendants especially to cater to the Indian passengers on board. All the international airlines hiring Indian flight attendants are looking for candidates with good communication skills, fluency in English, Hindi and a regional language. If you want to work for any international airlines based outside India, you may be asked to speak the language of that country.

Note: Knowledge is always good; so if you know any extra language, or are thinking of learning one, it will only serve as a bonus.

Myth No. 13: It is just a glamorous job

It is a job with lots of risks involved. The challenge already starts at the time of the interview. One has to perform extraordinarily to get this job. An interview may have hundreds of candidates and only the absolute best are given the responsibility of taking care of the flight and passengers' safety.

After the selection, one has to go through a period of intense training. The candidate has to clear many exams and assessments before he/she is allowed to go on board. Since it is a service industry, every airline has grooming guidelines, in order to ensure the cabin crew look unique in their uniforms, thus making them the face of the airline. Behind the beauty, there is intelligence, courage and hard work.

Congratulations!
You Have Got the Job! What Next?

After so much of hard work, undergoing multiple application and interview processes, you have finally got the job. Let's explore what happens after this and how it feels being part of an amazing industry, and working as a flight attendant.

Before you embark on your new career as a flight attendant, you need to go through intensive training. Some airlines give you a salary or an allowance for training, some do not; however, they may provide you with accommodation and meals. The training usually lasts for around 4-6 weeks. But the length of the training will depend on the airline, the aircraft in their fleet and aircraft variations.

During training, you can have lots of fun, but you need to put your best foot forward to excel at your job. You will learn about the following:

- Standard operating procedures
- Medical training
- Safety and security
- City codes
- Evacuation drills
- Duties and responsibilities of a flight attendant
- Product knowledge
- Service procedures

Be prepared to go through an intense period of studying. In

order to understand the entire curriculum and score the passing marks after each evaluation, you are required to put in a lot of hard work. You also need to have an impeccable attendance record.

The airline prepares you for many things such as safety procedures, customer service skills, providing first aid, inspecting the cabin, learning how to save yourself and the passengers in case of an emergency and so on. You need to be very attentive because you will be required to apply these techniques in real life situations.

The training is rigorous and continues throughout the entire day. It may start at 8 am and last till 5 or 6 pm. You must realise that you are in effect responsible for passengers' safety, and so the airline would want you to be perfect at your job. When it comes to being responsible for the lives of people, no chances can be taken. That's why such trainings are mandatory.

In the classroom, you will get to make new friends, and some of them will end up becoming your life-long friends. You will get to explore new things together, study, have fun, and live the dream.

However, please take your training very seriously. Airlines do not tolerate slacking in the middle of the training process or on the job. Failure to live up to the demands will eliminate your chance of living your dream job. Therefore, keep your eyes on the prize, and prepare yourself to work hard. You will be provided with a lot of study material and manuals to ensure you understand every bit of information. There is little to no space for mistakes when you're flying.

8 Important Tips and Strategies to Follow During the Training

In this chapter, we will discuss 8 important tips and strategies which will help you during the training.

1. **Eat, sleep, repeat** – You need to study for hours, and for that you need a lot of energy and concentration. Hence, after you get over with the day's session, you are advised to go straight to your bed to have a sound sleep after you've had your dinner and revised your day's lesson. Avoid hanging out with friends till late night.
2. **Make manuals your friend** – Keep referring to your manuals and try to absorb as much information from them as you can. Always keep you manuals updated and keep them handy.
3. **Budget your lifestyle** – Most airlines pay you a weekly allowance and some of them do so only after the training gets over. So make sure you spend money in such a way that you do not run out of it. Try to stick to a tight budget. Avoid dining at expensive restaurants, and going shopping unnecessarily. You may choose to shop once you have finished your training. Don't worry, you will have ample time and opportunities to do so when you start flying.
4. **Eat healthy, feel healthy** – It is very natural to fall sick due to changes in the food you eat or climate conditions. Choose what you eat carefully and try to stick to having food that you are sure will suit your stomach.

5. **Take regular breaks** – You are given a few breaks during the training session. This is the time when you can refresh and re-energise yourself for the next session.
6. **Form a group** – Studying in a group brings better results. You assimilate things faster when you discuss them with your study mates. If you have missed or haven't been able to understand something that was taught in class, you can always ask someone within your group to help you gain clarity.
7. **Watch your watch** – It is important to wear a watch to keep a check on time as you may be training in a different time zone. It is necessary to be punctual always.
8. **Dress for success** – You will be required to wear formal or semi-formal attire during the training. Pack according to the requirement of the job. During your job as a flight attendant, your uniform defines your identity. Here onwards, get into the habit of following a dress code, and maintaining consistency in your choice of attire.

Rest assured, you will receive all the information that you need to know from the airline once you are extended a job offer. They will take you through the entire process including what to pack and what to be prepared for.

The Probation Period

Once you successfully sail through the training, your probation period will start. The probation period is the time when the airline assesses you on different parameters to ensure your overall performance on the job. They check your adaptability to the fast-changing environment. They assess you on discipline, punctuality, and your behaviour towards passengers.

Generally a probation period lasts for 6 months. If someone falls short on fulfilling his roles and responsibilities properly, he may be asked to quit by the airline. Sometimes it may happen that you realise that this job is not suitable for you, and that you'd like to move on to something else. This is a trial period where both the airlines and the cabin crew test waters as they embark on a new journey together.

During your probation, you utilize all the skills you have been taught during training. That's why it is essential to spend a considerable amount of time understanding and grasping everything that is taught during the learning period. However, on-the-job training will teach you skills that no book can. You need to go through numerous feedback sessions, all of which have been designed for the single purpose of helping you improve in the areas you fall short in.

The probation period is not something you need to be worried about. You can live your life and relax. It is a time to make mistakes and correct them. Most importantly, enjoy the process. The fact of the matter is that you have got your dream job and you are living your dream life.

Some guidelines to follow during probation:

Time management – Always remember the importance of time. It is essential to show up 5-10 minutes before a scheduled meeting and perform all the tasks on time.

Availability on reserves – As we discussed earlier, the airline puts you on standby, and that is what being on reserve means. During this period, you are not on duty but the airline may call you if they have a shortage of operating crew.

Unhealthy office politics – Don't become a part of unhealthy group politics. Make friends with everyone and avoid getting into any argument, rumour-mongering, or gossiping.

Following instructions – During the flight, your seniors are there to assist you perform your duties, so follow their instructions. They are experienced and have handled many challenging situations during their career. You can learn a lot from them.

Obeying the instructor – You will be assigned an instructor for the in-flight training, so you are expected to work under his or her supervision. Display enthusiasm and finish all your assignments with your instructor on time.

Be a team player – This job requires you to work in a team. Be a good team player, coordinate well with your co-workers and work on having better relations with them.

Appreciation letters – Sometimes some passengers like to write appreciation letters for good customer service that you may have provided. Do collect them as it will work in your best interest during the meeting when your probation period performance is evaluated.

Showing patience – There will be times when you come across some passengers who are impolite and have some special demands. While handling such passengers, show patience and try to resolve their issue. If required, take the help of your colleagues or supervisor. Your objective, at the end of the day, should be customer satisfaction.

Happy you, happy passengers – A welcome smile is sure to change the mood of the passengers as soon as they come on board. Also, the atmosphere becomes pleasant and vibrant when people around us are smiling. A happy-looking face indicates that you love your job.

Checking the Roster

A monthly schedule of your flight is called a roster. It is published well in advance for the following month. It shows your flight timing, sectors, layover, reserves, and free days at home. And, it also shows the crew composition (the operating crew members).

You can take a printout of your roster and stick it on your bedroom wall or wherever you can easily access it. Mark your calendar. You need to do this so that you are well prepared for your flights and reserves in advance.

Layover Period

The layover period is when you reach a destination other than your base until your next scheduled flight. During this time, you are put up in a hotel, the accommodation charges of which are taken care of by the airline, and you also get paid for your food in the form of travel allowance.

During the layover period you are free from work and can utilize this time by exploring new places. However, you also need to save your energy for your next flight, so make sure you give yourself ample time to rest too.

My Journey

From being a small-town girl to becoming an international flight attendant

As I sit and ponder about my journey, I feel the absolute need to share how I became an international flight attendant despite being a small-town girl.

My purpose in sharing my experience with you is to make you believe that no dream is too big and impossible. When I had thought of becoming a flight attendant, it seemed like a hard-to-achieve dream because I had no exposure. However, I dared to dream big, and this is how my journey of becoming a flight attendant started.

My Life in a Small Town

I was born in a middle-class family in Shivpuri, a small city in Madhya Pradesh, India. Like most people, I had a carefree school life. I used to have short hair and would ride my scooty all around town, laughing and hanging out with my closest friends till we tired ourselves. I was the tomboy of the group – assertive, outgoing, and fun-loving. I loved sports and have even won a black belt at a state level karate championship at a very young age.

However, these golden days were soon to end. With the announcement of the 12th board results, everyone prepared themselves to join the rat race. The competition was tough and the stakes were high. A couple of my friends went out of town to pursue further studies. Despite faring well in my boards, my dream was to step outside the box, and carve a unique life for myself. I decided to complete my graduation from my hometown and then look for job opportunities.

One day while fiddling with the remote and shuffling through TV channels, I chanced upon a serial based on airline jobs. I got completely engrossed in it. I was so fascinated to see the takeoffs and landings, the work culture, cabin crew members travelling across the globe and living a glamorous life, that it became my source of inspiration. It matched with my dream of doing something big and different in life. Becoming a flight attendant then became my biggest obsession.

I could think of nothing but adding wings to myself so that I could fly high in the sky. I shared my dream with my parents. They agreed and fully supported me despite the glaring concerns of a few of my relatives and friends. They were opposed to the very thought and tried to dissuade my parents from letting me venture forward. As you might be aware, sometimes the biggest setbacks are caused by people who are considered to be part of your 'inner circle'. The goal, however, is to stay focussed on your dream and prove the naysayers wrong.

Once, there was a Miss College contest held in my college. One of my friends and I put up a food stall at the venue. While we were busy selling food, we heard an announcement that said that this was the final call for anyone who wants to take part in the contest. I had never thought of participating in that competition, so I didn't pay much heed, and continued selling food items at my stall. My mother had once asked me if I was interested in taking part in the Miss College contest, but I had said a firm no. I did not feel confident enough and was afraid people would make fun of me.

Nonetheless, after some time my name was called and I was requested to come up on stage. I was shocked beyond words. I looked at my friend, who was standing beside me. From her innocent smile, I could make out that she had recommended my name without informing me! She encouraged me or rather forced me to participate.

My family and friends boosted my confidence and told me I had a fair chance to win. At that point in time, I decided to believe in myself and have faith in God. Besides, I didn't have much of a choice but to perform. So, I decided to pretend it was just a game and nothing more. And guess what happened? Out of the 25 participants, I was declared the winner after clearing all 3 rounds of the competition. I was astonished when I heard my name being announced as the winner. For me, it was nothing less than winning a Miss India contest!

This experience taught me a valuable lesson – giving up is never an option, and complete belief in oneself is so, so important to winning in life. From that time onwards, my self-confidence increased and I learnt to trust myself.

I thought if I could win Miss College, I can become a flight attendant too. However, as the days passed my dream of becoming a flight attendant seemed to get buried due to lack of information and guidance.

During the second year of my college, my father's business suffered a loss and we had to face a sudden financial crisis. It was a tough time for my family. One day my father confided in my mother that he wished he had an elder son who could have supported them financially by being an earning member of the family. My sister and I had a younger brother and after getting to know my father's thoughts, something changed inside me. I wanted to become that son who could help my family financially and come out of the crisis unscathed. I knew then there was nothing more lucrative and rewarding than becoming a flight attendant.

Dreaming about becoming a flight attendant was only the first step. The next one was to figure out a plan of action to reach my destination. However, I was clueless. I didn't know where to start, who to approach, and how to apply for the job. In 2004, the internet was not so common, and in small town like Shivpuri, it was a rarity. Smartphones didn't even exist! The only sources of information were newspapers and career magazines.

One day I spotted a vacancy for a flight attendant's job in a national daily wherein they had mentioned their requirements and asked to send two photographs with a resume. To get a professional picture clicked, my hunt for a professional studio started. Finding a studio in our area was nothing less than a herculean task! Fortunately, I finally found one that did the job decently.

However, I had no idea how to present myself in the photograph. I still have that picture with me. Looking at it reminds me of how young, naive and clueless I was. How could I have expected recruiters to shortlist me? Although I was disappointed at not receiving an interview call, I didn't let it deter me from trying harder. In retrospect, the first setback only appears as a stepping stone.

Months went by without any update. Then I came across an airhostess academy. I called them up to inquire about the admission details and procedures. That single call made me nervous. I only remember saying 'yes' or 'no' and hesitating to speak more than two syllables. A quick conversation made me realise a few things: firstly, my English skills were poor. Secondly, I couldn't afford the fees. And lastly, I needed to work on my appearance.

Remember:

As Dr. Seuss, the great author once said, 'Why fit in when you were born to stand out?'

Without wasting time, I joined a spoken English academy to learn to speak English fluently, and applied for an education loan simultaneously. I was able to make quick progress in spoken English and moved a step closer towards my dream.

But life tests you at every point when you dream big. My education loan was rejected. The officer at the bank said that they would have considered my loan application had I applied to take admission in any engineering or MBA course. This was the first time they had received an application for an education loan of this type. In short, they were not sure if I could get a job after completing my course and repay the loan. I was shocked and shattered to say the least.

I could see my dream inching away and my family's financial crisis looming over our heads. When I came out of the bank, I saw a poster on a notice board that said: 'Give wings to your dreams with an education loan and we will help you get there', with phone numbers of the head office of the bank printed on it.

I called up their head office and somehow managed to talk to the head of the loan department, and shared my story with him. By God's grace, he understood my situation and assured me that he'll get the loan sanctioned. Within a month I had the loan approved. God was all set to take my test and make me stronger so that I could face further challenges.

Now, the last thing was to work on my appearance. I had to get my teeth aligned to have a beautiful smile. I went through a painful treatment. Every time I had to undergo a painful treatment for my teeth I kept telling myself, 'I would rather suffer now to enjoy later.'

In 2005, I arrived in Delhi and joined an airhostess academy. My mother came along with me. We lived in a room that was owned by a family we knew from Shivpuri. The place was also close to my academy. It was a very small room with no luxury. But what more could I have wished for? My mother fixed everything and returned to Shivpuri after a few days with a heavy heart, but with hope in her eyes.

I was all alone for the first time in my life. I had so many sleepless nights; cooking and eating all by myself was the most difficult part. I had never lived away from my family before. I had no television, no smartphone, no family members with me and no friends to talk to. Living in Delhi was not easy. The only thing that kept me going despite facing so many hurdles was my dream of becoming a flight attendant.

During my training at the air hostess academy, I had to go

through a taxing time, emotionally and financially. Many people criticized me thinking I was a very simple girl, and not cut out for a glamorous life. They believed I had little to no chance of getting selected in any airline. After hearing such discouraging comments, I used to get upset. But then I had promised myself to prove them wrong one day. My mother would always say that critics are there to make you a better version of yourself. So, despite feeling low, I would gather myself together, tell myself to ignore the critics and focus only on my goal.

Remember:

The genius is just sitting inside you; you just need to believe in yourself and let the genius in you come out to do the best.

Another thing that was proving to be a source of high pressure was getting a passport made. Having a passport is mandatory for the course. In those days, getting a new passport issued was not as easy as it is in today's time of super convenience. It took me almost a year to get a valid passport. Usually it didn't take more than 2-3 months. But in my case, everything was so 'special'.

I had to go back and forth between Delhi and Bhopal multiple times. Sometimes there was an issue with my present address, which was in Delhi, and my permanent address, which was in Shivpuri. Sometimes there was some issue with police verification. Oh my God! I cannot describe how difficult it was to get my passport issued. I used to get really mad and disheartened, wondering why all this was happening to me.

Finally, after all the hassle, I got my passport but sadly there was no vacancy for the next six months. After I finished my training from the air hostess academy, I was waiting for the placements with some airlines which the academy had assured us at the time of admissions. One day the placement head informed us that there were no openings with the airlines.

However, they offered to send us for interviews at five-star hotels. Needless to say, I was really disappointed. I was at my wit's end – paying the rent was pending, the EMI for the bank loan was supposed to start in a few months, and I had no job in hand. I realised I did not have the luxury of time to sit at home and wait for a vacancy to come up. Moreover, I did not want to bother my father with all the EMIs and expenses. I decided to take life head on and went for the hotel interviews. Out of 10 candidates, only 3 were selected and I was one of them. It might have been an accomplishment for others but it was definitely a compromise for me.

The most difficult part of the job at the hotel was the night shifts. The night seemed to be never-ending, with me standing in the lobby for hours, smiling and looking fancy all the time while feeling drowsy inside and hiding the stress and discomfort under smiles. It was not an easy task. There is a saying that after removing tons of dirt, gold emerges and the same was true in my case. I was promoted as a shift in-charge after 6 months of hard work.

Now when I look back, I realise that working with the hotel helped me get a lot of exposure and I learned a lot about customer service in the process. During my stint at the hotel, I appeared for many interviews for the job of a flight attendant but received only rejections. Travelling from one corner of the city to another for interviews and getting rejections was shaking my faith, leaving me completely dismayed. One after another, I kept losing my chance of getting selected with some of the most prestigious airlines in the world. I was low on patience and my much-sought-after dream seemed like an illusion.

I would cry myself to sleep every night. Those months were spent fighting against all odds, pushing myself to show up despite all the setbacks. They say when you believe in your dream and work towards it, the universe shows you a way.

Soon after, I saw an opening for an international airline in a newspaper. I sent the required documents and forgot about it. After about a month, I got a call from the airline's office requesting me to appear for the written exam. They informed me about the date and venue. I went there and appeared for the exam with very little hope of getting selected. Fortunately, I received a call after 10 days and was asked to come for the next round of interviews, which was followed by a group discussion.

When I reached the venue, I met several other candidates whom I found were experienced in their relevant fields. A few of them had already worked with some domestic and international airlines. This made me feel a little nervous. I had almost lost my confidence after meeting and interacting with them because I thought I was inexperienced and therefore not worthy of getting selected.

But as has always been the case with me, I managed to muster some courage and appeared for the next round and left for the day. To my surprise, I got a call again from the airline after a few days stating that I was selected for the next round of interview. This time my confidence increased and I started to hope for the best. From that day till the next interview, I couldn't concentrate on my current job.

For the next round of interview, we were put in a group of 3 and given a topic on which we were supposed to talk for about 2 minutes. And can you guess what the topic was? The topic was: 'What motivated you to become a flight attendant?' Here I found an opportunity to speak from my heart. I could have spoken for hours but there was a time limit of 2 minutes; so I had to restrict myself. I mentioned all the points that motivated me to become a flight attendant. That is where I got the chance to influence the interviewers and present myself as one of the best-suited candidates for the job.

Afterwards, we had a personal round of interviews with the hiring manager of the company. I appeared for the interview hiding my feelings of nervousness and the fear of rejection behind my smile. I was asked about customer service, and my knowledge and experience of working in the hotel industry came to the rescue, and I realised that no experience goes in vain. Everything happens for a reason. Even though I was unsatisfied with my hotel job, it was this experience that helped me navigate through the personal interview. After the interview was over, they told us that the shortlisted candidates will be called back for the final round.

'I want this job badly. This is my dream job. I can't let it slip from my hands after coming so close.' Such thoughts were crowding my mind. I couldn't sleep that night and kept imagining how it would feel to wear the uniform and work on board as an international flight attendant.

The next day I was back in the hotel, doing my regular shift—when you're on duty inside the hotel, cell phones are not allowed. Somehow, I took the risk and managed to keep my cell phone with me on vibration mode. This time I felt assured that I was going to get a call for the final round of interview. Doubts surely crept in but I kept them at bay and directed all my energy towards the takeoff. Finally, my phone began to vibrate. I could feel my heart racing. I ran towards the restroom in haste and answered the call. It was from the airline. The official on the other end said that I had been selected for the next round, which was swimming, and it would be held the very next day.

The Swimming Round – an Epic Story

My shift ended at 9 o'clock in the evening. The next day I was supposed to appear for my swimming round and barely got time to practice. I had learned swimming during my aviation course for 15 days only, and that too almost 2 years back. I had started to question my ability to swim and spent the entire night virtually recalling the strokes, and the lessons I had learnt 2 years ago.

The next morning, I went to the venue which was a five-star hotel. That day I saw all the finalists. They looked so confident because they had relevant experience. On the other hand, I was jittery.

We were asked to stand in a queue. One by one all the candidates before me got through with the swimming round. All of them aced the test. I was observing everyone in the hopes of memorising the techniques. Finally, my turn came and I jumped into the pool. I tried very hard to reach the end of the pool, but then I was going out of breath. So, I ended up stopping just before the finish line; I wish I could have done a few more strokes to get qualified.

Everyone else could finish the test and were asked to leave. I was still waiting there, disappointed with myself. The world seemed to come to an end for me. The examiner announced that I was not selected. I tried to explain my situation and requested her to give me one more chance, for which she refused. I didn't know what to do. Without giving it a second thought, I went into the pool again and started practicing for no reason. The examiner saw me swim and offered to guide me with a few swimming tricks. I immediately applied those tricks. Somehow, this gave my examiner some confidence in my swimming ability.

After some time, a group of examiners discussed something amongst themselves and one of them came up to me and said, 'You are a very passionate and hard-working girl, you didn't give up. So, we have decided to give you another chance. There is one more candidate who is missing today. So, we are going to conduct a swimming test again in four days, and you can reappear with her.' She wished me luck and left. I was stunned. I could not believe what I had just heard. Words didn't do justice to the gratitude I felt at that time. I started crying and thanking God. Suddenly, I remembered a few lines which I had read somewhere:

Believe in your dream. Never give up. When you want something badly, all the divine energy will appear to help you in some way.

Without wasting much time, I approached the swimming instructor of that hotel, said that I wanted to practice swimming for the next three days and asked if he could guide me to clear the test. He agreed. However, the instructor's fee was quite high because it was a five-star hotel.

I somehow managed that amount and paid the fees. I practiced for 3 consecutive days and made myself ready for the test. I became confident at swimming after that. I knew without a doubt I would be able to clear the swimming round. And frankly speaking, I could think of nothing for those 3 days except focussing all my energy on clearing the swimming test and getting the job.

On the day of the test, when I arrived at the hotel, another shock was waiting for me.

The pool was empty. We were informed that the pool was under maintenance. There was some miscommunication about the date of the swimming test.

I felt like I was back to square one. I had gathered enough confidence in the last 3 days, and was familiar with the dimensions and depth of the pool. Appearing for a swimming test in an unfamiliar territory was nerve-wracking. After waiting for a few hours, we were asked to reach another hotel for the test.

After reaching there, we found out the swimming pool was not heated. The instructor inquired with a few other hotels and found that there were no heated pools available in the city. Let me tell you that this test took place in the month of February in Delhi. We were wearing jackets and it was freezing cold! The examiner explained the situation to us and said it was completely our choice to take the test or wait until the next vacancy comes, after which we could reappear. There was no way I was going to take a chance especially when I had come so far. I informed her I was ready to appear for the test.

Despite the instructor's concerns, I decided to take the test in icy-cold water. One thing was sure: I was not going to back down.

I got ready and without thinking much, jumped into the pool. Just after a few seconds, my body became numb, and each stroke was a struggle. My body had started giving up, but my mind was its driving force.

There was a battle between my mind and my body. At last, I reached the finishing line. I made it. My passion made me a winner. I achieved my goal.

That moment is unforgettable and still motivates me to do the impossible and win the game of life. As I write this, my eyes are filled with tears. It's been more than 12 years since I had appeared for the swimming test but I still remember my body turning red and blue. After clearing the test, the examiner came to me and said, 'I can't even judge you on what you have done. I have no words. Only a person with a passion like yours could have done what you just did,' and she invited me and a fellow candidate to have a cup of coffee. After that she offered us a lift and dropped us at the nearest bus stop. While dropping us, she wished us luck for the last and final round, which was a medical test, which was due the very next week.

After appearing for the medical test, I waited eagerly for the final call from the airline. I spent a few nights imagining myself in the crew uniform, flying high in the sky and working on board. I wanted to tell the whole world that I had almost achieved my dream and I was just a step away to announce it officially. But I kept it a secret and didn't even disclose it to my parents. I wanted to give them a surprise. Those few days were terribly long.

On 22 February 2008, I received a call from the airline's office. My hands were trembling and my heart was thumping away. When I answered the call, the lady on the other side started having a regular conversation with me. At the back of mind, I wondered if this was going to be a polite way of rejecting me. After about a few minutes of our conversation, she congratulated me and informed me that I had been shortlisted to join the training slated to happen in a foreign country 13 April 2008 onwards.

At that moment, the world around me seemed to be a beautiful place. I was on cloud nine and experienced a range of emotions. All the hard work and sacrifices had finally paid off. The struggles and rejections I faced had taught me lessons for life and helped me become a stronger person. The pain I went through made me grow as a human being. All the experiences were blessings in disguise. Everything that had occurred during my journey, both good and bad, started making sense to me. It was finally time for a grand celebration.

I called up my sister and shared the whole story of my selection with the airline. Later, I told my parents and the entire family and my friends. We were all so happy and felt elated. Some of my relatives and friends who had little faith in my ability of becoming a flight attendant were in shock.

My life had taken off. It was time for a new beginning. I resigned from my job at the hotel and was absolutely happy typing my resignation letter while thanking each of my colleagues for the lovely experience I had working with them.

I was then called to the airline office to finish the paper work, sign the contract and fill some forms for the visa formalities. I was given flight tickets to the most beautiful place in the world to start our training – Switzerland. I was so excited to go abroad. This was my first long-haul trip outside India.

My father came to drop me at the airport. I had proven myself and became the son my father had always wished for. He looked so proud of me; I could see it in his eyes.

I went inside the airport to look for the airline counter. There I met the other candidates. After immigration and security, we waited to board the aircraft. I was so excited and nervous at the same time. I was entering into an aircraft for the first time and it was an amazing experience. I had butterflies in my stomach during takeoff. Till this day, words can't describe how surreal the feeling was.

Remember:

Your dream is waiting for you just on the other side of the shore; you just need to swim across with complete faith to achieve it.

After about 8 hours, we landed in gorgeous Switzerland, which I had only seen in Yash Chopra's movies till then. Something very special had happened to a very ordinary girl who had finally achieved what had seemed impossible to a lot of people. We were escorted to our hotel and given the keys to our rooms.

The very next day, our training commenced. It was insightful and fun. In comparison to the other candidates, I had to study much harder because for me everything was so new. Those 45 days of training were some of the most fulfilling days of my life. On weekends, we would explore the beautiful cities of Switzerland and roamed around like tourists. The country with its beautiful lakes, home to numerous mountains, and warm, friendly people, made the experience very special.

After clearing the exams, it was time to return to India. Now came the time for the real show – working as a cabin crew. I began to fly as a flight attendant and started living what I had till now only dreamt of. Despite the many disadvantages of flying, I take immense pride at honing my skills and being a flight attendant. According to a popular saying, 'Once a flight attendant, always a flight attendant,' and it seems to be true.

A decade has passed since I started flying and I still feel privileged. It is a wonderful job with a lot of responsibilities and challenges. I still enjoy flying and love my work more than anything.

Ever since I started flying, a lot has happened. I got married and have a son named Daksh, who is 6 years old and is equally passionate about aircraft.

I have got my dream job and I have decided to help hundreds and thousands of aspirants to achieve their dreams of becoming a flight attendant. By sharing my story, I intend to say, YOU ARE UNSTOPPABLE. Fuel your dream with good thoughts and hard work, and it will propel you to fly high. Chase your dream until you get it. Persist until you succeed. Don't worry about the hurdles. Keep moving ahead and I am sure you can become a flight attendant too.

Start doing these three things from now onwards:

1. Believe in your dream
2. Take massive action; do whatever it takes
3. Surrender your dream to the divine

You will receive help when you will need it the most. You will also be challenged every step of the way, and life will be a series of ups and downs. Be brave to accept the challenges and face them. Turn every adversity into opportunity. See possibilities in everything even when it feels difficult to do so.

Everything that happens with us is designed to push us to do better, to evolve and grow as a person.

If reading my story makes you work harder towards your dream, and draw inspiration and strength from my experiences, then I will consider it an achievement. You may be struggling right now but if you persevere you will come out stronger and achieve your dream of becoming a flight attendant.

Get in Touch

I hope this book can help you as a guide. Do share your experience by emailing me at megha.flyhigh@gmail.com. Make me a partner in your journey. Like my Facebook page (facebook.com/flyhighwithmegha) and be part of my Telegram and Instagram family @flyhighwitmegha. I will keep sharing valuable tips and strategies, vacancies, news, etc., which can help you get your dream job.

P.S.: For high usage words, some short dialogues, English drills to learn and practice English, you can email and request me to send an English manual and I will mail you a free copy as a gift from my side. I want to be a part of your journey and ensure you get all the help you need.

To receive information about relevant vacancies in leading airlines and the industry trends, please feel free to email me on the id I have provided above.

I will share tips and strategies that would help you stay motivated. I will act as a friend and mentor during this journey. Please remember to write, 'I commit to becoming a flight attendant' in the subject of your e-mail.